Chinese Lessons

Chinese Lessons

AN AMERICAN MOTHER
TEACHES HER CHILDREN HOW
TO BE CHINESE IN CHINA

Patti Waldmeir

ISBN-13: 9781981253258
ISBN-10: 1981253254
Library of Congress Control Number: 2017918716
CreateSpace Independent Publishing Platform
North Charleston, South Carolina

To Grace and Lucy, my gifts from China

Contents

Acknowledgments

SO MANY PEOPLE HELPED ME, shaped me, and most of all, tolerated me as I wrote this book. You know who you are, but in case you don't, I will name some of those who had the most to put up with.

First and foremost, of course, thanks go to Grace and Lucy, who as teens were probably just as glad that I was busy writing; it left me less time to nag them. Lu Mudan, our priceless Chinese nanny and my dearest Chinese friend, did all the cleaning and cooking and shopping and dog walking without which this book would never have been written. Shasha Chen, Zhang Yan, and Jackie Cai, my Chinese colleagues in Shanghai, were my invaluable guides to China and my much-loved companions as they helped me discover the motherland of my children. Colleen Zhang, our wonderfully efficient office manager, made sure the trains ran on time, as did Teresa Yan. My *Financial Times* colleagues and editors in Beijing, Shanghai, Hong Kong, and London taught me all they knew and made me laugh: Demetri Sevastopulo, Jamil Anderlini, Louise Lucas, Ben Marino, Geoff Dyer, David Pilling and Simon Rabinovitch had the worst to endure from me. Countless other China colleagues not named here also deserve my deepest gratitude. Dumpling and Huahua, our Chinese street dogs, did their bit, too, by walking me from time to time.

The Yangzhou girls—Lily Mueller, Natalie Petro, Maya O'Brien, and Emma Distler—are like my surrogate daughters. Their mothers and fathers and sisters and brothers—George, Leslie, Nick, Alex, Sophie, Frodo, and Sam Petro; Klaus, Tonia, and Maggie Mueller and Mimi; Nancy and Talia

O'Brien; Nancy Raff; and Joe and Morgan Distler—are as dear to me as family. Our Yangzhou family would never have hung together without the Muellers, who hosted almost every annual Yangzhou reunion at their weekend home near the Chesapeake Bay. Without Tonia's pancakes and crab cakes and Klaus's fishing lessons, the Yangzhou girls would not be like sisters as they are. The Petros welcomed us to Chicago when we moved there in 2016 and played hosts when the Yangzhou girls celebrated their joint eighteenth birthdays there in 2017. Rob and Maryline Sharp, fellow adoptive parents, encouraged me early on; if it weren't for them, I would not have Grace and Lucy.

Stefanie and Paul Taylor, our dearest friends in Bethesda, Maryland, where the girls spent their American childhood, were there to support me from the moment I got home from China with my first baby. Julia Bucknall proved a cheerful and exquisitely thoughtful companion on the trip to pick up Grace in China in 2000; she had much to endure from me on that journey.

So many *FT* colleagues over so many years helped me live the life that I always wanted: from Holman of Africa, my first mentor, to former editors Geoffrey Owen, Richard Lambert and Andrew Gowers: I owe you a lifetime of thanks. To Lionel Barber, current *FT* editor; Gillian Tett, US editor; Andrew Edgecliffe-Johnson, US news editor; and my dearest *FT* friend, Lucy Kellaway, I cannot thank you enough for all you have done. The *FT* gave me a crucial sabbatical to finish this book, the chance to live in the homeland of my children, and the opportunity to spend nearly forty years traveling the world and getting paid for it. Few are lucky enough to have such excellent colleagues, most of whom will have to remain nameless.

Shanghai friends like Maggie, Leo, Christine, Robert, Mary, Evan, Allison, David, Kathleen, Susan, Mark and various Jeffs and Geoffs kept me sane in that difficult city. John Fearon found Baby Donuts—what can I say? Carma Elliot provided invaluable insights into Chinese adoption, as did Jenny Bowen and Evelin Tai. Kathy Pauli, Constance van Neuss, Paul and Stefanie Taylor, Yong Lee and Leslie Petro spent time they didn't have to help me improve my manuscript. Clare Alexander encouraged and edited me early on; her selfless support was priceless. Todd Shuster, Justin Brouckaert, and Jane von Mehren suggested late changes, which were critical.

My late mother, Dorothy, and my father, Pete Waldmeir, taught me how to love my children. There is no greater lesson. My siblings Peter, Lindsey, and Christopher; my stepmother Marilyn; my aunts, uncles, and cousins; and my best childhood friend, Susan Waltersdorf, welcomed Grace and Lucy with a love that knows no genetics.

This book is not the fault of any of the people mentioned, but it is the work of many. You all have my most heartfelt thanks.

Prologue

It was a thing on one level so utterly mundane: a scrap of fabric tied with a rope, strewn in a dark cold alleyway, discarded. Except that the bundle was screaming: another abandoned newborn infant, fact of Chinese life for centuries.

This child was not my daughter, but she could so easily have been. My own two adopted Chinese children, Grace and Lucy, were abandoned at birth in an even colder winter on an even grimmer Chinese roadside. But I was not there when they were jettisoned.

I did not sense the presence of their mothers, breasts still leaking milk for daughters they would not be allowed to love. I did not look around for the father who had furtively placed his child behind a gate next to a wall in the shadow of skyscrapers. I did not find the bundle of their baby clothes, diapers, formula, and bottles, packed by a grandma or auntie, the only love note they could ever leave for a child they would never know.

But for this child, six weeks old and grievously ill with a heart defect, I was there to bear witness. And to grieve. A friend and I had stumbled upon her one December night in Shanghai, just after her parents had left her in the street. And as I clutched the nameless bundle, squirming inside the rope-tied bunting that swaddled her, I suddenly understood, as never before, the tragedy that is at the heart of every Chinese adoption. I wept then as I had never wept before: for her, for Grace and Lucy, and for all the other lost daughters of China. Previously, I had understood the pain of abandonment in theory; now I felt the burden of it, right down to the weight of this poor foundling's sodden diaper.

For in the split second that a relative put her down and walked away, this girl—and my girls—lost more than any adoptive parent can replace just by loving them. Brothers and sisters, ancient ancestors, all stripped off the family tree fractured by their abandonment. Name, birth date, nationality, ethnic identity, and family medical history, all gone, along with even the faintest memory of the past, the culture, the history they were born with.

These children—the baby in the alleyway and my own babies left in their own Chinese alleyways—are a unique accident of history. Sent by their country to live in nations all over the world, they are part of one of the biggest baby migrations in human history. Now they are coming of age, in parallel with the country that could not raise them. In the course of their lifetime, China's fortunes have been transformed: from a nation so poor it had to export babies to an economic hyperpower. China's orphans straddle that divide, between the China of then and the China of now, between the East of their birth and the West of their adoptive families. Bridging that gap—in their hearts, in their families, and in the societies that raised them—is a unique challenge, too.

The baby in the bunting was eventually sent overseas to live, just like my children. Her heart was repaired, first in the operating room and then by the love of American parents who raised money standing on street corners to adopt her. And when she joined her new family at age two, I was there. And I wept just like I did when she lay in my arms as a foundling: for all she had gained, but also for all she had lost.

Only the hardest heart could fail to be touched by how families like hers and ours are formed, but still, the shape of them baffles people. In the West or in the East, onlookers cannot help but wonder, "What's the old white lady doing with the two Asian kids?" The baby with the heart defect joined a Louisiana family that also has biological and foster children. None of us looks like anyone else's idea of family. We redefine the very notion of culture clash.

Grace and Lucy aren't what they seem, either. They are presumed Chinese until proven otherwise. In America, they are constantly complimented for how well they speak English, even though it is their native language. In China, they are expected to speak Mandarin perfectly and without an accent, though for them it is a foreign tongue.

They constantly surprise people, and sometimes disappoint them, because they do not look like what they are. Even their names scream cultural dissonance: Grace Shu Min Waldmeir and Lucy Helen Xinke Waldmeir, named for my Italian American mother, my Danish English American granny, my Swiss German American father, and the Mandarin monikers bestowed on them by their Chinese orphanages.

Are they American? Or Chinese? Or both? Or neither? Or it is healthier to pretend we don't even understand the question? Parenting across the culture line means making choices about ethnicity that most families never have to face. It was even a condition of the adoption that I vow I would never let them forget they were born Chinese. I didn't mean a word of it—then. But it has turned out to be the work of a lifetime.

When they were little, that meant teaching them to write their Chinese names, making them Chinese dumplings, and sending them to Chinese school on weekends. But as they grew, I decided this would not be enough. So when Grace and Lucy were seven and eight years old, we all moved to Shanghai to get to know the parts of ourselves that will be forever China.

This is the story of how that all turned out: the story of how two Chinese infants became accidental Americans in an instant and how their American mother spent the rest of her life trying to teach them to be more Chinese. The tale of how we all moved to China so that two girls who looked Asian but felt white could get the Orient deep into their bones and so that their old white mother could restore to them at least a shred of the cultural identity ripped from their souls when we all became a family. It is a memoir of how we moved halfway around the world, hit bottom as a family, and bounced back stronger. How we came to love first Chinese food, then the Chinese countryside, and finally, China on her own terms. How we learned to cherish it like a homeland—almost despite ourselves.

It is a tale of three women and two cultures, and of course, it is a love story. And to think this was all my bright idea.

CHAPTER 1

Learning to be Chinese in America

CHINESENESS WAS SOMETHING OF A cultural running joke at first. "Grace, Maya, and Natalie invite you to a 1st birthday party. Come or be a counter-revolutionary" read the invite when Grace and two of her orphanage mates celebrated their first American birthdays in November 2000. The girls and their American parents—all of whom had vowed in the same ceremony never to forget they came from China—honored that pledge by celebrating their birthdays together for years. This was the first of many Chinese-themed parties, and we started off in style: with a grainy print of a fulminating Mao Zedong, printed on thick cardstock. We celebrated our girls' Chinese heritage like something of a party gag.

So for that first birthday, I shoehorned Grace into a hip-hugging traditional Chinese *qipao* dress in midnight blue and paired it with a bright white Huggies diaper that she flashed in every photo. This was my attempt to genuflect toward her Chineseness: cheap brocade and frog closures, just like a pint-size Chinese courtesan—except that I never saw a child in China dressed like that.

But that was exactly the point. Chinese parents didn't need to dress their kids like Qing dynasty paramours to honor their ethnic heritage. For a Chinese parent raising a Chinese child in China—or the United States, for that matter—race just isn't a family issue. But for a pale parent like me raising an Asian baby, getting the ethnic bit right is tough. A cheap outfit from Chinatown was the best I could do to say "I love where you came from."

The cake on that first birthday was chemical-green frosting slathered over sections of molded Bundt cake, made to look like the lurid coils of a Chinese zodiac dragon. It was to be the first of many Chinese zodiac cakes: from dragon to snake, from horse to sheep, until we got to the Year of the Monkey, when my cake-making could no longer cope. After that we had rabbit-shaped cakes every year to mark the zodiac animal under which Grace and her orphanage friends were born. They couldn't possibly have cared less; it all tasted like cake to them anyway.

By the time Grace and her orphanage buddies turned three in 2002, they were dressing themselves, and no way were they going to choose *qipao*. It was all bridal veils and pink boas that year. Still, I soldiered on with the zodiac cakes: a rocking-horse birthday cake frosted in shocking pink and cornflower blue because it was the Year of the Horse in China.

Never one to buy a sheet cake when I could exhaust myself creating faux cultural ambiance in the form of a horse confection instead, I scoured the Internet for a cake recipe with four legs and a mane. But since birthday cakes shaped like zodiac animals are not, in fact, a Chinese cultural tradition, I could find no instructions for how to make a horse cake with Chinese characteristics. So I made one shaped like the kind of rocking horse they make in Guangdong toy factories instead.

Have I mentioned yet that this Chineseness gig had become something of an obsession? In some ways, it was just typical middle-class parental fixation on party themes. Given a choice between Cinderella or zodiac animals, I always chose the latter; it was so much less of a cliché.

Still, I sometimes sacrificed sleep, work, and unfortunately even playtime to this mania for kowtowing to their culture of origin. And the roots of that went back decades. By the time I adopted Grace and Lucy, I had already spent a lifetime, personally and professionally, pondering questions of race and ethnicity. From the time I stood, as a twelve-year-old, on the roof of Detroit's Tiger Stadium and watched the fires of the 1967 race riots burn down my hometown, I struggled to understand what it meant to be white and what it meant to be not-white.

So distressed was I with the racial fissures of the United States of my youth, the America of the Black Panthers and of Martin Luther King Jr's assassination, that I fled to live for two decades in Africa. There I nabbed a ringside seat as a journalist covering the unlikely peace deal between white and black in South Africa, one of the great race stories of all time. I taught myself five languages and lived in ten countries around the world, so fascinated was I with culture and how it shapes society. It was just never in the cards that I would treat my Chinese children like they were boring old white people. To me, they were ever so much more, and I wanted to make sure they knew it from the start.

Still, they were growing up in the depths of white America, and even if the cakes were foreign, the ambiance of our annual birthday parties for our Chinese daughters was all American, all the time. They did what real Americans do at parties: dip into the chocolate fountain once too often and clutch a vomit bag all the way home, tumble one another in piles of leaves, and slam into one another on the Slip 'N Slide. Or, as on their third birthday, take a rather improbable hay ride through the small western Maryland town where one of the families lived. No one stopped to ask why a passel of Chinese toddlers was riding down the main street of an apple-pie-and-opioids American town in cowboy hats.

We persisted in trying to create new traditions for this culture without a history, the family that is Chinese American by adoption. Every year, we had a party to celebrate Gotcha Day, the day our daughters were placed in our arms in China. We dressed them in Chinese clothes and fed them that year's zodiac cake, but we wove these exotic threads through the fabric of a traditional American summer barbecue. The girls wore brocade but munched hot dogs and potato salad. They ate cake loosely inspired by an ancient culture but topped it off with Popsicles. We were making this Chineseness stuff up as we went along.

I had only just dragged the Christmas tree to the curb, and it was time to start celebrating my kids' cultural heritage again. Grace and Lucy were three and four that year, so I plonked them down in front of a *Big Bird in China* video—I took the cultural commandant stuff so far that I scarcely ever let them watch television unless it had the pseudo-Chinese veneer of a Kung Fu Panda movie—and climbed on a step stool under the mock-Georgian fanlight of our front door to hang traditional Chinese New Year couplets.

It was hard not to tear the paper-thin couplets, but my main goal was just to avoid hanging them upside down. A Chinese friend had pointed out that hanging couplets was the kind of thing Cantonese restaurants did to make their sweet and sour chicken seem more authentic, not what middle-class homeowners did in the Maryland suburbs of Washington, DC, where we lived. She was born and raised in China, but she wasn't taking things that far.

Culture just wasn't the big deal to her that it was to me. But as I pointed out, there was a simple reason for that: my friend's child would learn to be Chinese automatically and by osmosis because her mother was born and raised in that culture and spoke its language to her. Her child would take Chineseness in through every pore, spending summers with Chinese grandparents, hearing Chinese on television, and seeing it on the walls of her home, even in suburban Maryland. My children would not. I could not speak to them in the mother tongue; I could not teach them its aphorisms; I could not live by its beliefs or even understand them. I had to make do with hanging couplets.

We even did our own Chinese dragon dance—with Maryland characteristics. After Big Bird got back from China, I put the girls down for a snooze and headed down to our dingy cellar to daub blobs of finger paint and stitch bells and baubles onto a ten-foot length of red cotton, with a chilled bottle of chardonnay to help the artistic flow. A houseguest from England had drawn a smiling reptile face onto a placard to be carried at the front of the procession, since the real papier-mâché dragon heads they used in China (or more to the point, at Chinese restaurants in America) scared the little ones.

Soon enough, the girls were up, decked out in matching pink brocade padded jackets and trousers trimmed with fake fur. They had an extensive wardrobe of mock-Chinese outfits in those days, sold cheap on eBay, they were always a hit with the kids, not because they were Chinese but because they were all about glitter and lace and shiny polyester. Lucy loved her bubblegum-pink brocade tank top with fuchsia net skirt for an outing to swing from the monkey bars; Grace's own idea of a school uniform back then was a series of velvet-bodiced, silk-skirted confections in different colors from eBay Hong Kong.

Back in China, families were traveling from far and wide to gather at lunar new year. And in our own lame way, we were doing the same. Other adoptive families were gathering under our roof to honor the five thousand years of history that our girls gave up to become Americans.

Grace and Lucy had an extensive wardrobe of faux-Chinese outfits

The festivities went on for weeks: Chinese New Year parties hosted by our local branch of the group Families with Children from China, which packed a couple of hundred people into a local Chinese restaurant; an annual get-together at the Chinese embassy just for adoptees; and a lunar New Year gathering just for single mothers of Chinese adopted children in the Maryland suburbs of Washington, DC (not as exclusive a group as it may sound).

Even the local preschool got in on the festivities. That's how I ended up standing in front of a group of four-year-olds doing something with a broom as part of the New Year celebration at Grace's school. But the concept of New Year ritual housecleaning was lost on them. They liked hearing an adult oink like a pig and squeal like a rat, according to the zodiac year, and no one turned down the red envelopes full of chocolate coins I gave them afterward—even if they were, in fact, Hanukkah *gelt*, since the traditional Jewish coins were the only kind that I could find.

By then I'd begun to wonder: why did I feel driven to be more Chinese than the Chinese? Many mainlanders don't know the nicer points of traditional culture since so much of it was destroyed by Mao Zedong, who thought communism had no room in it for culture. What was the point of me hanging New Year banners the wrong way up on a suburban home in Maryland? It was like mounting a single-handed Chinese cultural revolution against my own children.

I'd even made sure that at bedtime, many of the books we read had something to do with China: from *The Story about Ping*, a duck who loses his family on the Yangtze, Grace's hometown river, to our family favorite, *Daisy Comes Home*, about Mei Mei who had "the six happiest hens in China." I had basically bought out the whole Chinese children's book section of eBay. I even bought a series of early readers aimed at teaching simple Chinese characters to toddlers the fun way (as if there were such a thing). Any book about China, or adoption, or preferably Chinese adoption, I was all over it.

This wasn't an unusual reaction in my peer group of families with children from China. Entire businesses were built selling books and games and other Chinese cultural memorabilia to Americans. After all, none of us could ever have enough bedtime books; reading Curious George gets old after a while. And the kids couldn't have cared less anyway. They just wanted to delay bedtime.

They would clamor for a reading of *Daisy Comes Home* and cluck "Gu-gu-gu-gu-gu" along with Mei Mei, the hen's owner, as she tried to lure her chickens back home. Did they like that story, or did they just like the fact that I liked it? Toddlers are great people pleasers.

Would they rather have read all Little Critters all the time? Maybe, possibly, but I doubt it. To them, it seemed normal to have a lot of Chinese books on the shelf. We had them; many of their friends who were also adopted had them. They weren't in a position, as toddlers, to find that odd. Like kids around the world, my kids thought whatever our family did was normal.

I told myself I wasn't trying to teach my kids culture; I was trying to teach them pride. I couldn't tell my daughters how to be Chinese, but I could teach them to be proud of the fact that they were. Or that was my theory.

But over time I began to doubt whether all this pastiche culture really amounted to much. What was the point of stitching homemade dragon dance costumes using a friendly dragon head, instead of the traditional fierce one, to avoid scaring the toddlers? Why make my own moon cakes, as I did every Moon Festival, using a rustic wooden mold that no self-respecting mainlander would have in her kitchen and then fill them with apricot jam because my kids didn't like the traditional double-egg-yolk filling?

They loved having so many of their friends over so often, especially when it meant staying up past bedtime to parade around on the lawn swinging red battery-operated handheld lanterns. They soon figured out that the adults were too busy looking for the lady in the moon, the traditional character of the Mid-Autumn Festival, to worry about how many Big White Rabbit traditional Chinese toffees their kids had nabbed from the big bowl by the door. And as often happens in China, too, no one really ate the moon cakes. They were just there for show, a bit like fruitcake at Christmastime.

Were the kids even getting the message that they were Chinese? Or maybe they were just glad that, with two cultures to choose from, we were always celebrating some damned fool holiday or another: as soon as Moon Festival finished, Halloween arrived, and fast on the heels of Western new year came the lunar one. Throw in Gotcha Days and birthdays, and life was a constant party. None of it was all that Asian, though.

I was dimly aware that some adoptive parents fervently disagreed with what I was trying to do anyway. One parent even disputed whether the adoption group we belonged to should be called Families with Children from China since in her view our kids were really from suburban Washington, DC. She didn't want her child constantly reminded of where she came from, feeling that made her a kind of lesser American. She said she wanted her daughter to "feel like a real American and not a funny one."

My girls milked the whole ethnicity thing for all it was worth. They had twice as many parties as anyone else, and people gave them treats in the grocery store just for being Chinese. But I knew they would one day comprehend that they weren't just special—they were different. And to prepare for that day, I began to realize, they needed more than invented rituals and half-understood Chinese American traditions. They needed to learn Chinese. Heck, we all did.

It seemed indisputably the right thing to do: give them the best tool for understanding the culture of their birth, its language. We weren't tearing up our passports or renouncing the Pledge of Allegiance; we were just going to learn how to say *ni hao* with something other than a Washington, DC, accent.

That's how Grace ended up writing a thank you note in Mandarin to the caregivers at her orphanage in China. The note was written in oversize, rickety Chinese characters that looked in danger of tumbling from one line to the next, as though the childish hand that wrote them could not quite keep the bucking ideograms under control. The calligraphy lacked the customary Chinese restraint, but so did the sentiments, for this was a note written by Grace in her first year of learning Chinese to thank the orphanage nannies for looking after her so well as a baby.

I can't imagine what they made of it. They doubtless thought wiping her behind was just part of their job description. To thank them with a note like that was a profoundly un-Chinese thing to do. But I was more than thrilled that Grace had managed to write it.

She started slow, in the summer of her fourth year, with a spell at "Camp Happy"—not a Maoist reeducation project but a Chinese language and culture camp for American-born Chinese (ABCs) and kids like mine, who joke that they are really CBAs, or Chinese-born Americans. Run by two lovely middle-aged Taiwanese American ladies and held under the giant American flag at the local elementary school, Camp Happy's goal was to teach Chinese through arts, dance, games, and the distribution of plenty of cloying sweets.

Grace never learned a word of Mandarin there. But she acquired the basics of Chinese yo-yo (a traditional game that is mainly popular among Chinese septuagenarians), learned a few *gongfu* moves and became something of a camp mascot, since most campers were much older than the just-barely-potty-trained Grace.

Pretty soon, we were all spending Sundays learning Mandarin. By the age of five, both Grace and Lucy had an hour of Mandarin homework every day. Lucky for all of us, the school we attended—Rockville Chinese School, patronized mostly by second- or third-generation Chinese Americans who were no more Chinese than my girls—served a great lunch.

No egg foo yong on the menu there; it was far more authentic and delicious than the faux-Cantonese slop that passed for American Chinese food when I was growing up. They had the best dumplings I've eaten anywhere outside China and scrumptious Chinese fish-sauce eggplant, dripping in oil and spices. The kids liked the noodles, and I relaxed my usual no-candy-no-soda rule, so they could eat and drink what they pleased at Chinese school—so long as they said *xie xie* for it with a credible accent.

It took me a while to realize something was wrong with the props I had brought to that year's Rockville Chinese School lunar new year party. I'd pawed through the dusty jumble of a tacky Chinatown shop for cheap items to thrill toddlers with their Chineseness, grabbing packets of paper money with Chinese writing on them, stacks of red envelopes, and net bags full of chocolate coins wrapped in golden paper. I'd spent hours assembling them into new year *hongbao* packets so every child in the school would get one. But then the principal started hyperventilating.

Seems those bills with the Chinese writing were actually "money for the dead," the paper currency traditionally burned at the graves of ancestors during the Chinese tomb-sweeping festival every spring. Soon she was scurrying around trying to repossess every single dead note from kids who thought she was stealing their chocolate coins. And I and the other Chinese American parents were trying hard not to laugh, since most of them were born in the United States and were about as Asian as I was, if not less so.

By then I'd also helped start an after-school Mandarin program at the local primary school, which Grace and Lucy attended along with Chinese school on Sundays. And every week, I spent hours preparing their Chinese homework so it could be easily administered to a four- or five- or six-year-old by our succession of excellent South African au pairs, who came in every color except Chinese. And that's not counting my own Mandarin homework, because I was in the seventh-grade class at Rockville Chinese School myself.

Not surprisingly, I was at the top of the class since I was the only one who actually wanted to be there. I love languages. Studying them demands diligence, hard work, an ear for sounds, and a willingness to repeat mind-numbingly boring sentences over and over again. Just up my alley. I even drove around town listening to Mandarin tapes I checked out, again and again, from the local library.

But this whole China thing was taking way too much time. I had a demanding full-time job as a columnist for the *Financial Times* in Washington, DC, and I was raising two toddlers on my own in my fifties. Why did I think my life wasn't full enough already without teaching the whole family to speak one of the most difficult languages on earth—even if it was our mother tongue by adoption?

And Chinese Sunday school didn't seem to be working. Grace managed to win the Chinese speech competition in her second grade class, and Lucy, ever the diligent student, wrote her Mandarin characters in precise stroke order, just like she would have been forced to do in China. But neither could hold even the simplest actual conversation in Mandarin. They could scarcely tell whether the writing on the New Year chocolate coins was in Hebrew or Chinese.

And then, as so often happens in life, the opportunity suddenly presented itself to change all that. The *FT* informed me that my existing job in Washington, DC, was going to disappear and that I should think about alternatives. I tossed and turned through the wee hours of a November night, terrified of what that might mean for our family. Staying put wasn't an option. So where to? I had always planned for us to spend a few years in China. It seemed the obvious move for someone with a job like mine and kids like the ones I had accidentally ended up with. And anyway, wouldn't it be easier to learn Chinese there than in Rockville, Maryland?

By the time the *FT* editor suggested Shanghai the next morning, I had persuaded myself it would actually be the easy way out. We could have just skipped school or dropped Mandarin; instead we moved to China.

This wasn't the shock that it might appear. I'd been moving from country to country at the drop of a hat for years. My first big move in 1980 was to Ghana in West Africa—except that I actually thought, when the *FT* foreign editor first proposed it, that I was moving to Guyana in South America.

Normal people might be daunted at the thought of such a move, but I (arrogantly and, as it turned out, wrongly) prided myself on not being normal. Not having to do the next Rockville Chinese School homework assignment seemed like a bonus. What a relief, I thought. I'd never have to make another dragon dance costume or dumpling or moon cake; surely this whole Chineseness project would be easier once we could just buy our moon cakes in the grocery store like everybody else. And there would be no more bumbling around hanging couplets upside down and giving toddlers grave money. In China, I could leave the girls' Chinese cultural education to the experts.

Truth be told, I'd taken an instant dislike to China when I visited for the first time back in 1989. But I was quite sure that living there, I would grow to love it. By that time, I had learned to love cities from London to Brussels to Lagos to Lusaka to Johannesburg, just by giving them a chance for a few months. Surely Shanghai was no worse than Lagos on a bad day?

I wish I could say I gave the timing of our move long and serious thought. But the truth is that moving to China had always been a matter of when, not if. Still, I didn't think through just how hard it would be on all of us. By the time the girls got home from school on the day I had that fateful phone conversation with the *FT* editor, we were halfway to China in my mind.

The seventh grader who babysat for them after school was there, and they were already sitting down to their Mandarin homework at our vast square yellowwood dining room table when I told them, "Guess what, guys, we're moving to China" and rapidly followed it up with promising them a puppy. Grace claimed later that she thought we were moving to London (perhaps because that is where the *Financial Times* is headquartered). Lucy, then six, seemed to have little interest in the topic, whatever the continent. Put simply, they didn't know enough to be worried. Maybe none of us did. They didn't have the tools to imagine a life different from the one that we were then living, so they didn't even try. They just wanted to know what kind of puppy it would be.

Lucky for me, Grace and Lucy were happy, secure little girls who were not much given to worrying about anything, up to and including moving halfway across the globe. Even if they had been, I just plain wanted to do it. My brain summoned plenty of superficially plausible reasons why it was an indisputably good idea: language learning by osmosis (or so I thought), hot and cold running household help, a nanny who wouldn't total the car every six months, for the excellent reason that she doubtless wouldn't know how to drive. But I wasn't hard to persuade. I was bored with America and fancied a move to my children's motherland. I couldn't see how any of us could but benefit.

I doubt anyone who knew me was surprised. My family was used to me uprooting on short notice. My coworkers were all foreign correspondents, so they had a different definition of normal, too. And the other adoptive parents? Some said they wished they could do something similar, but no one questioned why I would be tempted. We all, in our different ways, wanted our children to understand their homeland; my way was just more extreme than most.

But my gut hadn't calculated the sheer volume of work involved in any transcontinental move, never mind one made by a single mother of two small children. I started small, heaping piles of indestructible bright plastic toddler toys by the curb with a big sign saying "Take Me!" Two fully equipped Little Tykes kitchens went out the door that way, complete with pots and plates and nauseating plastic food to eat from them. Three molded plastic toddler-size toy cars—the kind with a red roof and yellow doors and locomotion by pedal power—made it out the door that way, too. The inflatable toddler pool, with its blow-up palm tree, went to friends, and the creosote-stained backyard swing set sold to a neighbor who just happened to be a China scholar. Even two wooden high chairs that I had so lovingly stained with my own two childless hands for the children I would soon import from China had to be offered for adoption.

I was giving away their toddlerhood, but by then they were mostly done with it anyway; they helped me drag everything to the curb. The rule was anything you want to take to China, we will take. Nothing will be left behind unless you no longer want it. That's how the *FT* ended up paying for shipping a container full of moldy stuffed animals, My Little Ponies, and Barbie dolls to China.

But finding tenants for our 1930s colonnaded clapboard with its 1950s stainless-steel-walled kitchen and bathroom took a lot more ingenuity, not to mention capital. Stained powder-blue Formica countertops were easy to replace with faux-granite, and the stainless steel came off the walls easily enough. But the layout of the house was unforgivably pre–World War Two: the bathrooms were tiny and the closets even smaller, nary a double sink or walk-in wardrobe to be found.

And then there was the small matter of doing my full-time job, learning to speak Mandarin, and caring for my six- and seven-year-old children while also renovating a house that hadn't been touched for seventy years and selling most of the furniture in it. It didn't help that my primary after-school baby-sitter at the time was a twelve-year-old neighbor. She seemed the best option after her nineteen-year-old predecessor showed up blind drunk one day with her one-year-old son in tow and dropped a hot casserole straight from the oven onto the kitchen floor.

So by the time I found myself standing on our screened-in back porch on our last night in our empty home, looking out over the backyard with its grass

Patti Waldmeir

burned brown by having too many inflatable plastic water toys left lying on it for too many years, I was exhausted, terrified, and filled with something I could no longer pretend wasn't dread.

Grace and Lucy were still on a high about it all, fed by a constant diet of Leaving America parties: Grace's second grade class gave her an album immortalizing all the blond-haired gap-toothed friendships of that era; Lucy's first grade classmates wrote solemn good wishes and bound them in a keepsake book.

"We went to the Cheesecake Factory, and Piper gave me a necklace that was half of a heart, and she kept the other half, and my half was supposed to glow red if I ever needed her," Lucy recalled some years later.

"Weren't you upset to be leaving her?" I asked.

"No, why?" Lucy said. "I was too little. I just liked getting a present, I liked all the parties, and I liked being the center of attention. You said we'd get a dog, and I thought, 'Oh, OK.' I didn't feel anything."

Grace remembered performing in the school talent show the night before we left. "I didn't sing loud enough," was all she recalled. She had eyes only for the Game Boy she would be allowed to use the next day on the flight. It was her first electronic toy, meant as a bribe to behave on the tortuous journey. And then they cuddled up on my flanks and slept soundly until it was time to leave for the airport without any idea what was about to hit them.

I know they slept so well because I did not; my gut had recommended the move to China as the adventure of a lifetime. But my brain had finally realized I was moving with two little kids to a place where I didn't speak the language to do a job I knew nothing about and without sharing at least a fundamental human sympathy with the country I intended to make my home.

I kept trying to summon the arrogance of the long-time expatriate. I'd moved countries so many times in my life that part of me refused to believe it could be difficult. Lesser creatures might find it hard to uproot an entire life and plonk it down in a place they didn't even like, but not Flak-Jacket Bushwhacking Waldmeir, foreign correspondent par excellence.

But the rest of me feared I had made a terrible mistake. I began to worry that moving to China could be more than I could handle. And in the end, even that turned out to be an understatement.

14

CHAPTER 2

Of Crickets and Chardonnay

IN MY MIND'S EYE, I can still see the perky orange-and-white polka-dotted ribbon just as clearly as the day I picked it out of the remainder bin right before we left for China. I can practically still feel its grosgrain ridges against my fingertips, remembering how I congratulated myself on how easy it would be to spot that all-American bow, knotted around the handles of the six anonymous black valises that bore the weight of our whole lives to China.

But when we finally arrived, sleepless in Shanghai, there was nary a bit of grosgrain in sight on the luggage carousel. We'd just flown fifteen hours across half of Siberia without a hitch, but it seemed the pilot had forgotten all the luggage back in New York.

I'd had plenty of time to reconstruct a forensic mental image of those polka dots while everyone else on the plane mobbed the lost luggage desk. Chinese airline passengers are always the first into any lost luggage scrum. But I could scarcely dive in, elbows flailing, with two little ones in tow and virtually no Mandarin. So I hung back, looking down on the skirmish from a cultural high horse that guaranteed we were the very last to report our luggage lost, a good two hours after every other passenger was tucked in at home nursing jet lag. Only then did the fed-up and roughed-up luggage clerk turn his attention to the white lady with the two sleep-deprived Chinese kids. And that's when we really began to get nowhere.

"Describe the bags." I wasn't sure I'd understood his words exactly, but his meaning was clear from the laminated placard he was shoving in my face while miming that I should pick out the picture that most closely resembled my bags. But since they were black, oblong, wheeled, and zippered, there was no telling them apart from every other suitcase on earth, except for the polka-dot ribbon. Surely no one else tied the identical remaindered bit of grosgrain to their luggage handle, I thought.

But the clerk's English didn't stretch to *ribbon*, and my Mandarin couldn't make it to *polka dot*. So I looked into his almond-shaped eyes, and he looked into my round ones, and the gulf of incomprehension between us seemed unbridgeable. He assured me they'd likely turn up within the next week on their own, in any case.

So I gave up and did in haste what parents everywhere repent at leisure: I yanked my squabbling children, more roughly than I meant to do, and stormed off. We chose the "nothing to declare" channel since we not only had nothing to declare, we had nothing at all on our persons. And so at 5:00 a.m. on the first day of our new lives in China, we ended up in an empty airport, gazing out at a deserted taxi stand without so much as a company driver to meet us. (He had given up on us hours before.) We had no transport, no phone, and no idea of the Chinese name of our hotel, since I had trusted the company driver to know that.

I gazed out on the haze that passed for dawn on that typically smoggy Chinese day, across mile upon mile of what I then thought (and still think) is one of the least prepossessing urban landscapes on earth, and despaired of how we would ever even get out of the terminal, let alone begin our new life in China. I wish I could say that was the lowest moment of our eight years in the middle kingdom. I wish I could say that.

Lucy, then seven, was about a foot too short to reach the hotel hair dryer, so she had valiantly climbed onto the bathroom counter to unhook the dryer hose and was using it to blow-dry a pair of impossibly tiny Cinderella panties. She had just finished rinsing them out with a blob of hotel bath gel in a tub that was way too deep for her. They were the only panties she would wear for a week, while our luggage remained at large.

I'd been so proud of how I'd prepared for this eventuality—until it happened. I'd split up the essentials (my thyroid and asthma medications, the special cream for Lucy's persistent nosebleeds, and the anti-itch ointment for the mysterious rash she sometimes got on belly and ankles) among all six of the suitcases with the polka-dot ribbon. Divvying up the contents of a four-story six-bedroom house down to the last Q-tip and bottle of cold medicine and distributing them across the six bags meant to come immediately (and the umpteen boxes of our full-container shipment) had brought out the worst control-freak tendencies in me. I thought I had planned for everything.

Little did I know that advance planning is a skill I might as well have left at home. The middle kingdom knows just how pointlessly anal we Westerners are (none more anal than me); and China is never unwilling to demonstrate that fact, especially to newcomers.

That's how we ended up without so much as one spare pair of panties among us. Or, for that matter, a hairbrush for Grace and Lucy's waist-length straight black hair. Our carry-on backpacks had a couple of 1980s-vintage Game Boys—unearthed from the attic of the girls' honorary godmother, Stefanie Taylor, to be their first-ever electronic toys—and plenty of Super Mario cassettes. But the Sponge Bob toothbrushes were still on their round-the-world journey.

We asked how to get to the mall, not knowing how to say *Walmart* in Chinese, and were directed to the local luxury emporium, where we could easily procure a serviceable pair of stilettos or a bling bag but nothing so crass as a comb.

I knew the Chinese word for *hair*, and any idiot could mimic the motion of brushing it, since I had the kids on hand to use as demonstration dummies. But store clerks in China, especially those in the kind of small grocery where we eventually ended up, have neither the time nor the inclination to help anybody find anything, let alone people who can't ask in proper Mandarin (or preferably Shanghainese, the local dialect in our new home). I thought trawling the aisles would surely reveal a hair-care section; and it was probably as much a testament to my state of mind as to the shortcomings of the store's purchasing manager that I did not find one.

No brush for their tangled tresses; no comb to part their hair unevenly into pigtails; no hairbands to keep the tendrils out of their face; nothing to make us feel that life as we knew it had not, in fact, ended forever. Every package looked foreign, every food source appeared to have mysterious tentacles, and I couldn't even tell the difference between cornstarch and sugar or aspirin and laxatives. I had cash and even knew how to count it, but I could not even spend money competently in the homeland of my children. Eventually, we gave up, bought a dog's grooming brush, and used that for our first week in Shanghai. Try as I might, I still can't quite find that funny.

And that wasn't the worst of it: I had also needed a bra. But a fifty-something foreigner needing a fitting for her alien breasts—which, my children point out, have different color nipples from Chinese titties—made every clerk want to take a peek. I was in no mood that day to display what the shop girls of Shanghai clearly saw as my mutant appendages. I so wanted to find it all funny. But I seemed to have left my sense of humor behind with the luggage.

We couldn't even get a decent meal. Despite completing every teach-yourself-Mandarin course in the local library back home, I still couldn't even say "I want one of those" in Chinese. So we were doomed to eating tepid faux-Western food in the hotel restaurant instead of hot, fried Shanghainese comfort food from the street vendors just outside the door.

We came back from the dog brush store, watched some cartoons that were not improved one jot by being dubbed into Chinese, and settled in for our first night in China. The girls' giggles only barely penetrated the haze into which I sank after half a bottle of wine, a sleeping pill, and a couple of whiskeys from the hotel minibar. They were amusing themselves poking their little-kid fingers deep into my naked breasts, which jiggled entertainingly as we cuddled together under the vast expanse of the hotel's California king duvet. They were having fun, but I was idly wondering whether humans could actually die of culture shock.

Grace, Lucy, and the family cricket

My chardonnay and our cricket were my best friends back then. I'd promised Grace and Lucy a puppy as an enticement to move to China, but the new landlord did not approve. We'd moved into the three-bedroom apartment vacated by my *FT* predecessor, which had the virtue of convenience, and it had the right number of bedrooms and bathrooms (three each). Only later did I discover that it was also perched atop a vast underground construction site as Shanghai rushed to build new subway lines ahead of the 2010 world's fair. Our new home in the chic old European quarter of Shanghai was perfect in every way, except that it was surrounded by concrete, which tore the children's knees when they fell off their bikes, and we couldn't leave the house without risking beheading by a construction crane.

And the landlord didn't hold with puppies, so we set out to buy a cricket and find a place that sold something buttery, lemon yellow, and oak aged, preferably by the case. But locating a cricket in a nation that has kept them as pets since early antiquity seemed unnecessarily, nay unfairly, difficult that day. The mere sight of a taxi scared me in those early days, not because Shanghai taxi drivers were famously aggressive drivers, but because they aggressively refused ever to speak English (probably, not surprisingly, because they couldn't). So the trip to the cricket market began, as every taxi journey did, with me shoving a guidebook in the driver's face and trying to get him to acknowledge the address written in Mandarin therein. These days, Google Translate would have been my personal cricket shopper and made the whole thing painless. But back then, I seemed to be constitutionally inclined to find everything painful. Hence the fact that I had to stop on the way home to lay in a case of wine from one of Shanghai's few vintners.

Still, the portrait I took that day of kids and cricket is one of the bright spots in the dark night of my soul that was that first year in China. Lucy's hair has that crooked, single-mother-with-too-much-work-and-too-little-sleep part in it, and her purple oval glasses make her eyes look a bit crossed. Grace clutches a bit of lilac ribbon that just about matches her outfit: dangling from it is a bamboo cage that traps a lurid green stick figure. She could not look more delighted. I remember she didn't even mention how little it looked like a Labrador.

And that's the bit that breaks my heart: how brave my two little girls were while I was busy losing the plot in Shanghai. Grace and Lucy disliked China from the outset. They complained that it was dirty, which, compared to antiseptic Bethesda, Maryland, our American home, it indubitably was. (Cleanliness is overrated, I say.) They spluttered with outrage when some old fart lobbed a gob of spit, as Shanghainese old farts are wont to do, in the direction of their flip-flop-clad feet at the bus stop. And they complained about the bus too, since at home we had a capacious seven-seater minivan, crammed with all the things we never needed in Shanghai, like inflatable dolphin pool floats and portable croquet sets. And the local 7-Eleven didn't even have Slurpees.

But while I was numbing my woes with pinot grigio and cricket music—cricket song, wine, and Ambien made a mean insomnia treatment—they were out trying to make the best of things. So within a day or two of moving in, they had made friends with Xingxing, the daughter of the migrant worker family that ran the cigarette shop at the mouth of our lane.

"Xingxing's family pees in a bucket." Grace had raced home to report back from the front lines of the real China that the neighbor family not only had no bathroom, they did not even have a toilet. "And they all sleep on one big hard bed with just a sheet over it." Her eight-year-old voice squeaked at the mere thought of squatting over a bucket to do her business and sleeping on a plank instead of a bunk bed. Our apartment had three bathrooms, one for even the littlest of us. And though she shared a bedroom with Lucy, at least they each had a bit of stained and pitted foam mattress to call their own.

But the little the neighbors had, they gave without reservation to my children. Unlimited free sodas and ice cream from their shop and even one day, as a special treat, a lighter in the shape of a handgun, which the kids used to set toilet paper on fire. I wasn't sure how to point out, in a culturally appropriate fashion, that in America my kids weren't allowed to play with fire and that we were trying to avoid dairy right then, since China was in the midst of a poisoned milk crisis that would sicken three hundred thousand babies. That's not something I had learned to say at Rockville Chinese School.

The girls' relationship with Xingxing was not all devoid of culture clash. At one point, Lucy refused to play at her house on the grounds that "It stinks." Xingxing's family ate a lot of fish, which gave the house an odor my picky American daughter did not appreciate.

But the lure of free ice cream and dangerous weapons apparently overcame the scent because the kids were soon off back to the tobacconists, where pushing on the back wall of the display case revealed a hidden staircase that climbed past the bucket to their one-room home upstairs.

Grace and Lucy made it very clear they were glad not to live like that—even for all the Bic lighters in China. But eventually, they got over the bucket, and what they remembered years later was how Xingxing's petite, pretty, thirty-something mother knew how to style their Chinese hair so much better than boring old white Mom did. And that she accepted them for exactly who they were: Chinese kids who, at the time, could hardly speak a word of Chinese. That wasn't always true outside the tobacconist shop. And that was something about this whole Waldmeirs-to-China gig that I simply hadn't banked on.

"Do they know they're adopted?" From our first taxi ride to our last in China, every driver asked this. Usually the question came sotto voce, in case the children had perhaps not noticed up to then that their hair was straight and black while mine was curly and light, their noses were flat whereas mine was hooked, and our skin tones were shades of pink and yellow that could not possibly have been produced by the same gene pool. Cross-racial adoption isn't the kind of thing that anyone can keep secret for long, but China's taxi drivers were willing to believe that I had somehow managed it.

But once we let on that we understood Chinese, they would really get warmed up to the topic: "You two girls should be very grateful to this foreigner for adopting you. She is a wonderful person, and you owe your lives to her." Thus spake the taxi drivers, the pedicurists, the hairdressers, and the hotel clerks of China. With one voice, they lectured my children on the life-long duty of gratitude they incurred the day I decided to pluck them from orphanage obscurity. Chinese people may not look alike, but they definitely think alike on the topic of adoption: only saints do it. The only proper reaction on seeing a foreigner with Chinese children is genuflection.

I have always liked more than my fair share of attention, so I took all this gratuitous adulation in stride. It's doubtless one of the things I liked best about living in China. I was not just unique; I was also deemed to be morally superior to the average human, simply by virtue of adoption.

Back home in America, total strangers may have assumed that I chose adoption at least in part because of the opportunities it offered for instant canonization, but they didn't say so. But in China, people came right out with it. They said that no one in their right mind would adopt across the color line (or, for that matter, at all). "Your heart is filled with love," they would invariably declare. "These children are very lucky to have you."

That always provoked a bit of he-said she-said in which I would insist that I got more than I gave out of the bargain, while the taxi driver or hairdresser or random stranger would assert ever more stridently that I was, in fact, Mother Teresa. Eventually, I would suggest a truce to allow that all three of us were really rather fortunate to have found one another.

I remember having exactly the same conversation while soaking naked in a rosewater hot tub in our neighborhood spa, standing in line to ride the wooden roller coaster at the local amusement park, letting tiny fish eat the dead skin off my feet at a nearby beach, getting a full body mud rub at the massage parlor, and ordering Shanghai's famous soup dumplings at the greasy spoon (make that dirty chopstick) near our house. No one ever chose to discuss the weather.

One Thanksgiving, when we sat down for sweet potato casserole topped with caramelized marshmallows and an outrageously overpriced turkey at the home of American neighbors, we were all asked to come up with something plausible that we were thankful for that year. I made the mistake of suggesting that I was grateful for the gift of my precious children. The family's Chinese nanny wasn't having it: "You can't say that." She seemed outraged. I assumed I'd made a grammatical mistake, but no. "They can be thankful for you, but you can't be thankful for them," this normally mild-mannered servant insisted. "It's not possible for a parent to say they are thankful for a child," she explained. Talk about a culture gap.

This was China's attitude toward Grace and Lucy from the moment we set foot on mainland soil. And though they said "Yes, ma'am" and "No, ma'am" in all the right places, the girls hated these primers on filial piety, that most Chinese (and least American) of cultural concepts. They seemed tempted to tell China where to put Confucius.

I can't—and won't—pretend to know what Grace and Lucy were thinking about all that, deep inside. Adoption had been, from the start, so much a fact of life in our family that we never noticed the differences between us unless some tactless taxi driver pointed them out. And then we didn't care much. At least I didn't think so at the time. Grace and Lucy were little, and they made a point of ignoring most everything adults said to them anyway, whether it was "Brush your teeth" or "Honor the old lady." I mostly remember the time that one driver asked me if I nursed them when they were babies; that kept us all laughing for days.

Indeed, adoption itself was a bit of a running joke in our family. It wasn't something we spoke about in hushed tones or a topic we tiptoed around. Over lunch at our local McDonald's in Shanghai once, Lucy asked me, "Mom, why did you adopt us?" And as I took a deep breath and began to muster a sensitive and age-appropriate reply, she answered her own question: "Because you were old and ugly and lonely and naggy and wanted some children to nag so you adopted some, woo hoo!" she declared with glee. And then she fell off the chipped plastic stool, laughing so hard she dropped her french fry.

I once dragged the following admission out of Grace, who could always smell a serious conversation coming a mile away and would normally deflect into silliness: "It bothers me that it bothers other people."

And Lucy chimed in, "People pity you." Clearly the taxi drivers of Shanghai did, but Grace and Lucy never seemed inclined to pity themselves about it—at least back then, when a trip to McDonald's atop a double decker bus and the challenge of trying to jump high enough to touch the electric wires overhead was all it took to delight them.

Lucy's nose had just begun to bleed, and it seemed there weren't enough tissues in China to stem the red tide of her nostrils. Our new nanny, Lu Mudan, was rushing for more as I cradled Lucy on my lap, encouraging her to lean forward while I pinched the bridge of her nose, hard, to encourage clotting.

Mudan—who, in her sneakers, T-shirt, and athletic shorts, looked far younger than her fifty-something years—looked confused. She spoke no English, and I couldn't take time to look up the word for nosebleed, but the source of her confusion rapidly became clear. In China, parents tilt their children's heads back when they have a nosebleed, and in America, they tilt them forward.

This was cultural dissonance of the most tactile kind: whose home remedy should prevail? The culture that birthed her or the culture that raised her? We decided to try it both ways: I tilt this way; you tilt that way. Then let's see which works better. That was the day I knew what a gem I had found in our Mudan. China is not a flexible place, and most Chinese nannies would simply have lacked the confidence to suggest such a creative solution. She would be with us for all our eight years in China, Chinese mother to my children and best Chinese friend to me.

Mudan made our house seem like a home when nothing else about Shanghai seemed homey. She spoiled them—and spoiled their eating habits for life—by cooking different meals for different children and indulging Grace's voracious appetite for meat, carbs, and never a green leaf ever.

Grace and Lucy had been dragged half across the world, torn from family and friends and native language, and plonked down in a city they did not like as part of a cultural reeducation project they neither agreed to nor approved of. But Mudan didn't spend time pitying them; she just raised them. And she protected them from the taxi drivers far better than I ever did; she just shut them up with one cold stare. If a taxi driver asked whether they knew they were adopted, she just pretended his lips weren't moving.

But it wasn't just taxi drivers who were asking my kids constantly to explain why they were not what they appeared. On their first day at their bilingual Chinese-British school in Shanghai, the teacher, understandably enough, asked where each kid was from. "The other kids were saying, 'Half Chinese and half Finnish' or whatever, and they got to me, and I said, 'I dunno, Chinese American adopted sort of, I guess?' And everyone was like,

'OK, that's a bit weird,' and moved on to the next person, who just said 'French.' It was like there was supposed to be one right answer, but I didn't know what it was," said Lucy.

In a school essay that year, Lucy pondered that same question. "When people ask me where I'm from, it's hard for me to answer because they are right by blood I am Chinese, but I did not grow up in China. Me personally I feel that I am both Chinese and American but in different ways. I feel that I am American because I grew up there and my first language is American English. I feel that I am Chinese because I look Chinese, I have Chinese birth parents, and for the first year of my life I lived in China. People in Shanghai always just assume I am Chinese or that I have a Chinese Dad. So when Shanghainese people ask me where I'm from I just say, 'it's complicated.'"

Even ten years later, Lucy said she always felt like something was not quite right. "It was like there was something off about me. I looked Chinese, but I couldn't speak Chinese fluently back then. I felt American, but I didn't look American. I felt like I was disappointing people around me."

"At the time I was a kid, and I didn't really care," she said. But the memory of it endured.

Grace, for her part, claimed to have only two memories of those early days in Shanghai, and neither had anything to do with either being adopted or being Chinese: "Antoine gave me a baffle gun in third grade. Everybody was playing with them, and I didn't have one, and he said, 'Here, I'll give you one to get you started,' and I was so happy. And then there was the time when Hannah D. and I were crying on the playground. I think we'd had a fight or something."

For of course, most of their time was not spent listening to filial piety lectures from taxi drivers; it was spent playing softball at school, pining for a puppy, or fishing for stuffed animals with the electronic claw at the local arcade. It's remarkable how normal their life was, given we had left an entire lifetime of 7-Eleven Slurpees back in America.

This had all seemed like such a good idea, back when I was baking fake moon cakes in our Bethesda kitchen. Surely living in China would benefit my girls on every level. Learning Mandarin would give them a foot in both the cultures that would compose the two-superpower world of the twenty-first century, understanding Chinese people would make it easy to work in either country when they grew up, and more fundamentally, living in China would give them an avenue to access the lost culture of their birth. The secrets of Chinese culture, history, and ethnic identity would unfold before them as they put down roots on mainland soil, I imagined, and if they ever wanted them, there were brothers and sisters, aunts and uncles, family medical histories and ancient ancestors to discover on the mainland, too. The possibilities seemed endless—and endlessly appealing.

But it had never occurred to me that Grace and Lucy's experience of China would be profoundly different from—and in some ways, exactly the opposite of—my own. Where I was a bit of a rock star, they were seen as just two more Chinese children among millions, only less so. They were only unique when in my company; on their own they were Chinese nobodies. Or as Grace would put it: "Mommy, they treat me like I'm Chinese!" And she didn't appreciate that I thought that was funny.

My plan had been to make Chineseness at least available to them as adults by bringing them to live in China as children. But I began to see that might be tough to do, anywhere and at any age. "Their peers who stayed back home and went to events where Chinese culture is carefully packaged around holidays like moon festival or Chinese New Year find it easier to be proud of being Chinese than my girls do," a friend with adopted daughters once told me. "Here in China they realize there is a lot *not* to be proud of, too."

Still, this was exactly the kind of cultural education I had wanted them to get: a profound and deep warts-and-all knowledge of their homeland. It was so much better than hanging couplets upside down, so much better than playing with money for the dead, so much better than apricot moon cakes. And best of all, they were getting it all by osmosis; knowledge of China and what it means to be Chinese was seeping into their pores every time they visited Xingxing at home or watched how Mudan comported herself on a public bus. They were learning about the real China; and it was all happening without me having to lift a finger. Or so I thought until I began to realize that China might, in fact, be the hardest place on earth for my girls to learn to feel

Chinese. Because nothing could be more obvious in China than just how un-Chinese they were at heart.

But I was too overwhelmed with work, the quotidian difficulties of life in China, and communicating in a foreign language to spend much time figuring out what to do about it. I figured we'd give the China project a year to prove its worth. In the meantime, I just reached for more wine splits from the hotel minibar and doubled my dose of sleeping pills.

"I PROMISE I WILL NOT GET MARRIED AND LEAVE YOU IN SHANGHAI." I had written this in block capitals, and taped to the wall next to Grace's lower bunk a few weeks after our arrival. She wanted to be able to see it there at any hour of the day or frightening night. We'd brought the bunk beds from home: hand painted in white and spackled unevenly with purple paint, complete with the smear of lilac in the wrong shade at one spot where it didn't belong.

They were the only beds my kids had ever slept in, and the mattresses were familiar, right down to the old bedwetting stains. But though the room looked like home with all the same old furniture in it, it took Grace years to get comfortable in it. The transition to Shanghai was much harder on her as the big sister; she was just the right age to think that being brave for Mommy and watching out for Lucy were things that could reasonably be expected of her. But she'd had a powerful lot of trouble managing that.

So within weeks of our move to Shanghai, she developed an obsessive fear that I'd run off and get married, leaving her alone to look after then-seven-year-old Lucy. "How will I get Lucy back to America?" she had asked, leaving me almost speechless with remorse for the fear I'd inflicted on her, just to introduce her to her roots. I used my usual trick of defusing with humor, pointing out that she was more likely to be hit by a direct nuclear strike than see her mother go out on a date in China (or anywhere else for that matter). But she was not reassured to hear me talking cavalierly about nuclear incineration; she wanted the promise in writing.

So I rooted through plastic drawers crammed with every conceivable shade of magic marker, finger paint, and construction paper to pull out a sturdy sheet and a thick black pen to write out the promise that tore my heart with guilt: "I PROMISE I WILL NOT GET MARRIED AND LEAVE YOU IN SHANGHAI." And then I used the same thick, solid, authoritative black marker to write a list as long as her eight-year-old arm of the phone numbers of every relative, friend, neighbor, or schoolmate either of us could remember in America and taped it to the side of our fridge. And to the day we left China, I updated that list from time to time, with the names and cell phone numbers of Shanghai neighbors whom Grace could call in an emergency—though I never did elope, in lieu of a nuclear meltdown.

Then it was Christmas, our first in Shanghai, and that brought more painful snapshots of how much she was struggling. She will doubtless reveal more of that old angst one day to lover or therapist. But what I heard that first Christmas was enough to be getting on with, from a guilt-stricken parent's point of view.

It was Christmas Eve, and we were all trying to pretend we didn't mind spending such an emotive holiday in a country that thought of Santa Claus primarily as a marketing prop for selling luxury goods. We'd bought a sad, spindly potted evergreen about the size of Grace and overloaded it with all the decorations we'd previously lavished on a full-size conifer. We'd declared Christmas a holiday—though it wasn't a day off from work in China—and invited our favorite American friends over for a Christmas Eve of games and comfort food. Chinese American Evelin Tai and her two children, Karis and Elijah, roughly the same age as Grace and Lucy, came to be with us, and a good time was had by all.

But when the Tais went home, about 10:30 p.m., Grace and I got into verbal fireworks over her plan to stay up and watch a bootleg DVD, not least because I still had hours' worth of Christmas presents to wrap in my role as single-parent Santa. It was one of the worst arguments we've ever had and ended in tears on both sides and a complaint from Grace: "It was a lot nicer at home," my valiant child flung angrily at me, knowing how much of myself I had invested in making China palatable for her. "You're a lot more crabby, and you're always tired here," she said, standing with her feet planted wide apart on the cheap Berber carpeting of her bedroom, which unaccountably made me feel even farther away from home, where all our Bethesda floors were tasteful hardwood.

I'm not proud to say I responded with a burst of guilt-ridden sobs and a wholly unwarranted complaint that she should not say mean things to me on Christmas Eve. Knowing she'd hurt me—the last thing that preteen Grace ever wanted to do—she started quickly dialing back. "Mommy, I understand, you have to work a lot harder here, so you're more tired, and that's *why* you are more crabby here," she rationalized as we collapsed in a cuddle on the rental-unit carpeting that reminded neither of us of home. She fell asleep trying to be brave, and I went to bed heartsick for the burden on my children of being raised by a single mother who had no one else to turn to on a lonely Christmas Eve in a hostile city in an alien culture that I simply could not figure out how to love.

CHAPTER 3

Sleepless in Shanghai

"IT'S LIKE YOU WENT A little bit crazy." Eight-year-old Lucy had fled into a corner of the kitchen, back near the storeroom where I kept my wine stash, as I fulminated at her about something that, years later, neither of us could ever remember. But we both remembered what happened next: I grabbed one of the many pairs of reading glasses I had scattered throughout the house and snapped them in two—in her face. I didn't touch her, but I scared her. The look on her face that day will reproach me forever.

I repented instantly, carting her off to the corner convenience store with its vats of alien soy snacks and battle-ax cashiers, promising her any treat in the store. She chose Skittles. I chose a Suntory lager. Something to take the edge off all that guilt.

Those were the days when I was still Lucy's favorite person: the lap she always wanted to occupy, the bed she would feign fever to spend the night in. That night, big sister Grace was away on a Shanghai Girl Scouts' outing, so it ought to have been special for me and Lucy. Normally, the presence of Skittles and the absence of Grace would have been her idea of a perfect combination. Instead, that night was a low point of our lives together and of our lives in China.

Throughout our first year in Shanghai, I became more and more disconsolate, more and more depressed, and more and more irritable with the children. And I blamed most of it on China. I powerfully wanted to fall in love with the place, but I simply couldn't. And the girls—in the name of whose cultural education I had upended life as we knew it—took the brunt of my frustration with their homeland.

By then, we had our luggage. We had enough brushes, combs, and hair ties to clog an entire chest of pastel plastic drawers on the bathroom counter, and the dog brush had been retired to the keepsake box, where I hoped it would one day make me laugh. They were in school, I was at work, and Mudan was in the kitchen. What was not to like about China?

I found plenty. I was disgusted to find myself acting like the worst kind of expatriate: the kind who refuses to accept a country on its own terms and faults it for being, of all things, different from home—duh. "No one begged you to come to China," I kept reminding myself. "If you don't like it, go back."

Like anywhere on earth, China is a jumble of qualities, admirable and not; of people, charming and not; of places, beautiful and not. In those early days, I only had eyes for the "nots," and that, obviously, was far more my fault than China's.

Most of all, I disliked the way Chinese people treated one another. Everybody seemed to love babies—or more precisely, their own babies or grandbabies. The streets were full of grandparents adoringly caring for toddler grandkids. But the circle of human sympathy in China seemed to me an unnecessarily narrow one. Immediate family mattered a lot, extended family mattered more than in the West, and friends and even colleagues were astonishingly loyal. (I will cherish my handful of Chinese friends, including Mudan and my charming and talented colleagues, Shirley, Zoey, and Jackie, for the rest of my life.) But perfect strangers just didn't count much. I was told it was a Confucian thing. If so, it's hardly a great advertisement for Confucianism.

For a country with one of the most exquisitely nuanced cultures on earth (and five thousand years of practice), the sheer coarseness of daily intercourse between strangers shocked me. Drivers were brutal to moped riders, who were brutal to bike riders, who were brutal to pedestrians, including those pushing baby strollers, if the baby wasn't related to them. Passengers boarding the subway forced their way on, while those inside the car forced their way off. And my fundamental sense of the rational order of the universe was just plain offended by how so many people strong-armed their way onto elevators before anyone could get off.

As I learned back at the luggage scrum, most of this was just healthy scarcity behavior. If I'd spent high school dreaming up ways to denounce my parents in the Cultural Revolution and never had a full belly without a ration coupon until I was thirty years old, I'd probably barge onto elevators, too.

But the fact is, I didn't, so I wasn't prepared for it. I grew up in a land with an overabundance of elevator space and no need to fight for it. From there, I moved to a continent that certainly has no shortage of brutality to its name—Africa—but where daily life was still chalk and cheese to China's. In Ghana, my first and favorite African home, people apologized to me if I fell over in the street, even when it wasn't their fault. It took a while to get used to a chorus of "Sorry, sorry" from onlookers, whenever I tripped. I never figured out if Ghanaians were apologizing for the state of their roads, the state of my shoes, or the simple fact that life is hard, no matter where you live it.

In China, I once tripped on the pavement and ended up skinned and bloody in the street, a circle of passersby ogling me, some even laughing. No one offered me a hand to get up. Rationally, I knew that wasn't what it seemed; if they helped me, they might be blamed or even held legally responsible for my fall. There were highly publicized cases of that happening in China. I also knew that some cultures laugh when embarrassed or afraid. My brain knew I shouldn't take it personally, but my heart felt they were just plain cruel. Those were the moments that made it hard to love Shanghai.

I smiled at people, and most chose not to smile back. I tried to chitchat about the weather, and most seemed to think I should read the weather report. I'd brought along my American cultural assumptions about what were appropriate forms of idle conversation, and I unpacked them along with the spare panties. It's a wonder I didn't expect everyone to wish me a nice day.

And then there was the Bird Lady. She lived at the mouth of our short lane, and I had to pass by her to go to work. Every day I greeted her, and every day she pretended she hadn't heard me. She had a black mynah bird in a cage; one would think that would have gotten the conversation going. And it did: between me and the bird. He hung in a cage outside her door, and every day, he would tell me, "You are very beautiful," while his owner did nothing but glare. I wanted to weep.

Eye contact was another issue for me. In most countries, it's possible to forge a bond of shared human intimacy just by smiling at someone's baby. But in Shanghai—which is a lot like New York, a city I don't like much either—that didn't work. Few people had even the slightest interest in idly passing the time of day with a stranger.

Doubtless that's what's made China great: the single-minded determination to spend every waking hour bettering one's condition in life. I remember being told by a trash picker, in my first few weeks, that he didn't have time to be interviewed for an article I was doing because he'd lose too much income in the five minutes he spent talking to me. But that wasn't an attitude that won China any popularity contests with me.

It didn't help that, during our first winter living in Shanghai, I could never get warm. That was about culture gap, too: most Shanghainese have never met an open window they don't like. But Americans like me, raised before the 1973 oil crisis, believe in never putting on an extra sweater when they can jack up the thermostat instead.

So I hopped in one of Shanghai's mercifully cheap (but unmercifully scarce) taxis to go out in search of a hot-water bottle. At the local Carrefour, famous for its gargantuan line and gratuitously unhelpful staff, I tried to mime my way to the part of the store that specialized in warming people up in winter. By then I knew how to say *hot* and *water* and even *bottle*, but the Shanghainese shop assistant in the canary-yellow Carrefour uniform shirt had me rattled, so it didn't occur to me to combine them. So I acted out a charade that included boiling a kettle, uncorking the water bottle, pouring in the liquid and snugging it all up in a knitted cozy. She was not finding this either amusing or informative, but she eventually asked languidly whether I wanted a *reshuidai* (which literally means "hot water bag" and is more correct than calling it a bottle anyway). Every day was like that for me while I was getting used to China: a huge expenditure of unnecessary effort that got me where I needed to go in the end, exhausted.

I was simply overwhelmed by how alien it all was. Most of this was just the usual expat angst and was in no way the fault of the middle kingdom. I simply didn't have enough Mandarin to solve the little dramas of daily life.

I once made the frosting for Grace's birthday cake using cornstarch instead of confectioner's sugar because I couldn't decipher the Chinese characters on the box.

"Wow, Mommy, it's getting thick so fast," she said. I ignored her. She tasted it. "Yuck!" she said.

"Don't be silly. I'm sure it's fine," I retorted. We ended up having to chip the hardened white paste out of the food processor. Only Grace thought it was hilarious that we'd tried to frost her cake with liquid concrete.

And part of my problem was also simple loneliness. On our first visit to the Sino-foreign hospital where we would thenceforth procure all our medical care, I was required to give an emergency contact in China. I didn't have one. Not one. I asked a Chinese acquaintance if she could act as first point of contact in an emergency, just to alert my company to take over, and she made very clear how little she liked that idea.

And what's more, I realized that I couldn't even competently tell a taxi driver how to get to the hospital in a city where ambulance service was nonexistent. That frightened me so much that I assembled Mandarin cue cards for every possible hospital we could ever need to visit in any corner of Shanghai and carried them around with me for years. I was wracked with guilt at having brought my children to a country that not only had no public safety net, no Chinese equivalent of 911, but no private one in the form of a network of friends either.

I'd been living like a foreigner all my adult life, but never quite so much of one as I was in those early days in China. Not Mobutu Sese Seko's Zaire, not Robert Mugabe's Zimbabwe, not a Zulu kraal or a black South African township in the midst of a firefight had ever seemed as alien to me. I'd lived my life on the basic premise that we're all the same under the skin, and China was the first place I'd ever lived where, for the most part, that just didn't seem to be the conventional wisdom.

Race is a concept so deeply rooted in the Chinese soul that when many Chinese look at whites—or teach their children to look at whites by pointing at them and labeling them loudly as *laowai*—they don't see people who are basically the same under the skin. Maybe we all do that, and I just noticed it more in China. But Lu Xun, one of China's most respected philosophers, put it this way: "Chinese people see foreigners either as gods or barbarians—never as equals." That made me feel lonely in a way I'd never felt lonely anywhere else on earth. I hoped it was like stinky tofu (or, for that matter, Roquefort cheese): something I could get used to, eventually.

Surely it wasn't time to get up. In fact, not only was it too early for the cheap windup alarm clock on the bedside table to trill, it was also Sunday. But it wasn't the alarm that had wakened me; it was the drilling. Drilling was illegal in Shanghai before 7:00 a.m., after 10:00 p.m., and all the time on weekends, but no one was counting. I woke to it, and I fell asleep to it. So I grabbed up the kids and headed out, just past 8:00 a.m., to escape the inter-cranial surgery element of the average Sunday in a flat in Shanghai. And on the landing outside our flat, we ran into our neighbors, chased out into the streets by the noise.

Renovation racket: it was the thing every expat (and not a few Chinese) loved to hate about China's economic miracle. But it wasn't just the buzzing that got me; it was the powerlessness. I had the law, the management, and the neighbors all on my side. But no one could stop the drilling.

At work, I had a translator to render things into English for me but no one who could make China make sense to me. And more to the point, I didn't have the personality to thrive in a world where clear rules were made and then just as clearly ignored.

Within a week of my arrival, I'd discovered that there were no clear procedures for things that were heavily rule-bound in other countries: paying tax, transferring funds into the country, or renting office space. The *FT*'s accountants told me they couldn't give me a clear read on my Chinese tax liability, and they couldn't quite explain why not, either. I ended up paying taxes through a Chinese accountant who filed my returns in a far-flung suburb of Shanghai where I neither lived nor worked; no one ever explained to me how that could be legal.

Then I discovered that Chinese exchange controls would make it impossible for me to bring in enough money to pay my Chinese taxes and my rent, let alone any living expenses. Surely not, I opined. Surely so, I was told. I'm not going to disclose how I squared that particular circle, but suffice it to say that any country whose legal code prevents law-abiding visa holders from meeting their obligations of tax and rent doesn't deserve to know how I managed it.

And finally, I discovered that though our office lease would run out soon after I arrived, no one could tell me where it might be legal to look for new premises. Journalists like me were tightly restricted in China. My savviest colleagues in Beijing advised that I just go ahead and sign a lease and deal with any problems afterward. In fact, old China hands constantly told me to do just that: act first and ask for permission afterward. They found it liberating, but I couldn't think of anything more frightening.

By the end of the first few weeks, I was wondering if China and I had irreconcilable differences. My personality—rule-abiding, forward-planning, borderline control freaking—could not have been a worse match for a world where there may have been rules, but everyone except me enjoyed ignoring them.

Even that old stalwart "Green means go," for example: it didn't work in China. I learned to teach the kids not to walk when the green man said walk and not to stop when the red one said halt at street corners. They were better off just crossing the road first and asking questions later. The kids loved having an excuse never to wait for the light to turn red, but I found even simple actions like that utterly terrifying. Lucky for me, and for them, I eventually realized that crossing the road whenever you damn well please is great fun. But that took years.

I also felt constantly judged—and found lacking—in the area that meant most to me, care for my children. All winter long, Shanghainese passersby commented disapprovingly on Grace's attire, or lack thereof. Until her teen years, she insisted on wearing only shorts and a T-shirt, no matter the weather—even during one trip to an ice festival in northern China when the temperature was 25 degrees below zero Fahrenheit.

Oversensitive as always to our public image, I took to carrying a heavy fuchsia-pink Gap down jacket everywhere we went, not because I was subject to any illusion that she might actually wear it but to head off the notion that foreigners adopt Chinese children just to inflict frostbite on them. Left to ourselves, I couldn't have cared less what she wore. I'd bought that down jacket at a yard sale in America for five dollars, not wanting to waste any more on a garment I knew would never be worn. My parental logic was that it was really more her business than mine to decide if she was cold, and if cold, she would put on more clothes. End of parenting issue.

But in public, I always felt that I was playing a role that went far beyond actually preventing frostbite. I had to prove that I wasn't neglecting her, that I loved her as much as a biological child, and that I could parent her as well as any Chinese mother. The spotlight that I loved so much in other circumstances became a searchlight when it came to parenting in public. And Grace and Lucy knew it.

One particularly frigid Christmas Eve, as we were doing last-minute shopping on Shanghai's premier shopping street, Nanjing East Road, then-ten-year-old Lucy decided it was time to tease Mommy. Gesturing at her then-twelve-year-old sister clad only in gym shorts and short sleeves, she intoned melodramatically in Mandarin to anyone who would listen, "Look at this poor girl. Her mother won't buy her any clothes to wear; isn't it a crying shame?" We all collapsed in laughter; what better fun than taking the piss out of other people's views of our unusual family? But that incident brought home to me, like nothing else could, that there was a flip side to our charmed life in China. We were never out of the spotlight; we always had to act like rock stars. And the truth is that I wasn't always up to the task.

Lucy was on an inflatable mattress squeezed between my platform bed and the mirrored glass doors of my closet. So I couldn't creep out that way. On the other side was Grace—I was using the kids as hot water bottles at the time, and it was her turn for the coveted spot on Mommy's mattress—so I couldn't get out that way, either. But I needed more drink.

I'd woken in a panic over whether I could ever get used to China—that happened almost every day back then—and the bottle I always kept by the bedside was empty. Could I risk taking another Ambien? I'd already had one and most of a bottle of wine. Or was it two bottles? Must have been closer to two if I was even contemplating taking another Ambien. It was 5:00 a.m., and I was desperate to grab two more hours of sleep before the school alarm went off at 7:00 a.m. I decided more chardonnay was the ticket, even if it did mean I might still smell like fermentation the next morning.

So I padded barefoot across the cool tile floor of the kitchen that Mudan kept so spotless, past the spot where I snapped the glasses in Lucy's face, to the fridge and its ever-present bottle of amber comfort. I splashed some on the counter as I filled the oversize wineglass to the brim—Mudan would clean it up when she got there the following afternoon—and stepped squeakily across Lucy's inflatable. Lucky the kids always slept so deeply, I thought. They had no idea what I was up to.

But of course, I knew exactly what I was doing when, after that huge glass had not knocked me out, I poured another one at 6:00 a.m. And then another one while standing in my pajamas at the window, watching them wait by the road for the school bus because I surely couldn't stand with them after drinking all night. But I had no idea what to do about it. One night, I feared, I would lose count of the glasses of wine I'd downed and then lose count of the Ambien. And then those little girls would wake to something unspeakable in the bed beside them. In a foreign country that was their motherland but certainly not their home.

I'm told that depression, and for that matter excessive drinking, are common reactions to a transcontinental move. But I'd moved countries no fewer than eight times in my life by then; I figured I ought to be better at it than the average expat.

Half of me had always secretly despised trailing wives who couldn't cope with moving the odd ten thousand miles without falling apart over it. But I found myself doing exactly that. And mimicking them in another way, too: breaking the traditional expat rule that alcohol should never be poured until the sun is over the yardarm. My nautical grasp of the term, which apparently means no booze before noon, had always been hazy, so I thought it meant no drinks before sundown. I dispensed with that rule in Shanghai, telling myself that it was hard to know when the sun went down anyway, due to all the sky-scrapers and the smog.

I was bored and isolated; wine was my only indulgence. Of course, parenting two children on my own had always been a fairly isolating experience. From the time they were toddlers, I worked at home, slept when they slept, and came to think of adult interaction as what happened when I paid the cleaning lady or ordered coffee from the McDonald's drive-through. And that was even before I came up with the bright idea to expose us all to culture clash.

As much as anything else, I was physically exhausted. I soon became obsessed with the notion that a good night's sleep would help me cope. But the only way I could get to sleep was to drink and drug myself into a stupor first. Which is how Lucy and Grace ended up in my bed after sleeping in their own beds for all their lives up to then. I expect it had something to do with fearing I might not hear them if they called out in the night. And yes, I know that's not what Mother Teresa would have done.

By the end of that first year, when my sleeplessness was compounded by a bout of jet lag after our first home leave trip to the United States, I knew I was in trouble. My chest was tight with anxiety from the moment I started work in the morning until I came home to start the daily losing battle with insomnia. Anxiety-fueled asthma made me breathless, and that fed my sense of panic. Small wonder I found it hard to sleep and even harder to imagine what had ever made me think this whole China lark was a good idea.

My bare arms were covered in a thin patina of sweat, and greasy hair stuck to the back of my head because I'd been too exhausted to wash it for days. I'd run down to the corner convenience store, where tall, cold Suntory lagers dripped condensation and sold for two renminbi per sixteen-ounce can. I'd run out of wine, so I'd left the children asleep in their beds to buy beer to get me through the night.

Writing about that time from a distance of years, my mind's eye looks on with a mixture of shame and incomprehension as I watch myself counting coins onto the Formica counter to pay for lager when I ought to have been cuddled up next to my daughters at home. Later that night, my hand slipped from the metal corkscrew as I uncorked a bottle of cheap wine, sending the bottle opener crashing into my cheekbone where it would leave a bruise that took weeks to disappear.

All these years later, I still have one sore cheekbone, and I'm glad. I don't ever want to forget the terrible last fortnight of our worst year in Shanghai. I don't ever want to forget standing on the broad windowsill in their bedroom and watching through the gap between two apartment blocks as they waited for the bus. I knew they were perfectly safe. Other children their age walked alone all the way to school or took taxis solo. But I never again want to see any sight as sad as those two children standing on the side of the road without me. I never want to let them down like that again.

So Shanghai showed me just how low I could go as a parent. And everything I tried failed to help me climb out of that hole: antidepressants didn't work; therapy (at the hospital where they still wanted to know who my emergency contact person was) had little impact. Adding Xanax certainly didn't improve things.

As the first anniversary of our move drew near, I pondered whether we should just jack in the whole *Roots* escapade and go back to Rockville Chinese School on Sundays. I didn't want to leave. I didn't want to stay, but most of all I didn't want to fail. I didn't want to give up on that part of ourselves that would forever be Chinese. But I had given myself twelve months to decide, and now that deadline was imminent. I became, if anything, even more despondent.

But as I poured my woes down the cell phone line to my brother Peter in Detroit, he pointed out that there was nothing sacred about a year, no immutable law of the universe that said I must let the calendar dictate something so existential. "Why not give it fourteen or sixteen months and then decide? You can always leave then if you still hate it."

And though he had never lived in China, never been to Asia, and doubtless had no idea why I'd ever moved us there in the first place, that turned out to be exactly what I needed to hear: take the pressure off, give yourself a break, and go with the flow. If you're meant to be there, eventually you will know it.

I had help from our kindly family doctor from Vermont (a longtime China hand); I got sympathy and counsel from a Chinese American therapist who was struggling as much as I was with the alien-ness of her ancestral home, but most of all, I got support and wisdom from a meditation group that I would attend almost daily for the rest of my time in Shanghai. In that group, I found friends, I found calm, and I found tools for coping with life on its own terms. How odd that I had to move halfway around the world to learn to do something so simple. But as the Chinese say, "When the student is ready, the teacher appears." I was finally ready to learn to love China.

And that is how our first year in Shanghai ended: with me learning a lesson I ought to have learned long ago but could only grasp when brought fully to my knees in the middle kingdom: to accept the things I couldn't change (China), to change the things I could (my reaction to it), and to know that I could never survive in my children's homeland until I let it be exactly what it was. I started putting my clothes on for the bus run again. The girls went back to sleeping in their own beds. I didn't break any more reading glasses.

Every day, I would sit cross legged on a porch swing near our house, breathe in great lungfuls of smog-clogged air, and breathe out my arrogant sense that I could ever change it. And I meditated on the unlikely sound of birdsong. I realized that when you have ears only for drills, all you hear is drilling, but even in Shanghai, even with twenty-three million people, even in winter, there were also birds singing. I still had plenty of beefs with the motherland, but I learned to nurse them from then on over nothing stronger than coffee—and birdsong.

CHAPTER 4

The Race for Grace

FOR DECADES, I HAD PINED for two little girls named Grace and Lucy. But in my dreams, they were not Chinese. China was the place you got to if you dug too far down in the sandbox; it was not where babies came from—at least not when I started wanting to be a mother.

That was probably circa 1962, when like the rest of America's second graders, I was crouching under a desk during the Cuban missile crisis. The Grace and Lucy I dreamed of then were white. My husband (in the dream, I had one) was some kind of a military guy. I, too, was in the military. (Both my parents had been.) I dreamed of going to the base hospital to birth the kids, but not about how I would conceive them in the first place. That turned out to be a lot more complicated than in my reveries.

It was my birthday. I spent them all the same way from about age twenty-nine onward: trying to figure out how I was ever going to get married, or more to the point, get my hands on a Grace and a Lucy. That particular year, I was out hiking in the South African highveld, where the red earth, the sage-green bush, and the startling splash of a lilac-breasted roller bird were the only anti-dotes I knew to the pain of childlessness, spinsterhood, and general existential crisis. I wore my cracked old leather ankle boots, the ones with the frayed red laces and the layer of dust from spending every weekend therapeutically hiking the gullies and canyons of South Africa.

I gnawed on that pain throughout my thirties, most of which were spent covering the end of white rule in South Africa, first from Zambia, exiled home of the African National Congress, and then from the home of apartheid itself. Marrying my live-in Jewish South African boyfriend, David, seemed like the best plan for much of that time. He made me laugh, he was brilliant, and we loved to cuddle up at night and listen to books on tape together. That seemed more than many couples could say. But we never did tie the knot, and eventually I moved on to become US editor of the *Financial Times* in Washington, DC. I was a member of the elite White House press corps, which meant I could hang out in the West Wing within feet of the Oval Office, but I couldn't summon the energy to make my bed in the morning. Because every day, the chances diminished that I would ever have Grace and Lucy.

That's how I ended up sitting in a room at the back of a suburban strip mall with six other people, trying to grieve. I'd finally realized that the only way I could become a mother at my age would be by scoring a baby through adoption, and in 1997, when I came to that epiphany, that meant a baby from China. But it seemed the price for that was to emote on cue.

The adoption agency's counselors wanted us to grieve for our failure to conceive a child the conventional way. Strictly speaking, that wasn't my problem. I didn't have an infertility issue; I had a matrimonial issue. But if grieving for failed fertility was part of the bargain, I was all for it.

I had thought fleetingly of test-tubing it. But I wanted a baby, not a chromosome carrier; it seemed to make more sense to love a child who already existed than to create one in the lab. I can honestly say my motives were entirely selfish. I wanted kids, so I set out to get me some. I wasn't in it to save them; I wanted them to save me.

China was the obvious source. There were plenty of abandoned Chinese babies, they were mostly healthy, the process was straightforward and quick, and the kids were supposedly abandoned, so no one would ever come looking for them. Still, the first adoption agency I chose took the view that they all still deserved perfect parents. They rejected most of us after the mandatory grieving session. Our anguish, apparently, was not of the approved variety.

A life of bitter spinsterhood and existential barrenness loomed ahead of me. Until one day, I took a call from Rob and Maryline Sharp, two of the other grief-session participants. They had decided to try again with a different agency. If they could do it, perhaps I could, too.

Without knowing it, we had all chosen exactly the right time to adopt internationally; no time before or since would have been better. By some remarkable accident of both female hormones and geopolitics, I was ready to adopt at exactly the moment when China was most ready to let me do so. Before that time, China had not been a major baby exporter, and it has not been one since. (US adoptions from China rose from almost nothing to peak at nearly eight thousand per year in 2005, then fell to around two thousand a year within a decade.) And crucially, China was one of the few countries that allowed older single parents like me to adopt healthy infants.

I'd already babyproofed my life; how could there be no baby wanting to stick her fingers in all the electric sockets I had plugged with little plastic outlet covers? I'd chosen a house that was way too big for me but just the right size for baby, au pair, home office, and basement rental apartment to help finance it all. I'd put all my assets in trust and given up my stressful job as US editor. I was working from home in a job that would give me five months maternity leave per child and time to have breakfast, lunch, and dinner with my kids. The only thing missing was the kids. And at forty-four, I was nearing the upper limit for Chinese adoption.

It was then or never. So when the Sharps—a couple I barely knew—called with details of two new agencies they had found, I was finally desperate enough to listen. And half an hour later, I was in the offices of the International Children's Alliance adoption agency, talking to the people who would eventually make me Grace and Lucy's mother.

The message from ICA's miracle-working China coordinator, Junji Chen, and its warmly supportive adoption adviser, Sue Orban, was clear: getting a baby from China was a piece of cake. Rejected by another agency? Just don't mention it. Almost past the upper age limit? Don't mind the rules; the Chinese certainly don't. Worried that China won't give a baby to a journalist? Just call yourself a "financial editor." Too late to get two? Apply for two at once and take staggered delivery. They had a workaround for every hurdle, even the last one: What sane person would give me a baby in the first place? Ms. Orban, an adoptive mother herself, reassured me that however flawed I thought I was, it just wouldn't be enough to put China off. I walked in fearing

I would spend my life a crotchety old spinster. I walked out thinking spinster, definitely; crotchety, probably; but maybe not childless. Hallelujah.

I rode the Hallelujah train right down to the District of Columbia police department to get the first of a series of documents attesting to the fact that I had committed, among other things, no ax murders in any of the many jurisdictions I had lived in. England? Nothing to report. Belgium? All clear there, too. Ghana, Zambia, South Africa, France, Italy: no complaints. Since there was nothing I loved more than a checklist, I had my adoption documents assembled in a matter of weeks, despite operating in only the penumbra of the Internet age.

Ms. Orban strongly advised I apply for two babies at once to save on processing time. If I had not heeded that advice, I would not have Lucy. China subsequently made very hard for forty-something spinsters to adopt healthy infants. I only got her because I was already on the waiting list.

All that was left was the required home study, done by a local social worker, who interviewed me about my childhood and then made an appointment to come vet my Victorian in the trendy Dupont Circle neighborhood of Washington, DC. Predictably, I was quite sure she would find this million-dollar home inadequate to house one small Chinese orphan. I decided to fall back on that old ruse, fresh brownies in the oven to fill the house with the smell of motherhood, although I instantly confessed that the brownies were meant as a bribe. She didn't hold it against me.

I failed to mention, on the other hand, that the building's basement, backyard, and alleyway were infested with rats and that I regularly trapped a handful before my first cup of tea in the morning. Nor did I point out that I'd found a dead one in a glue trap beneath the rocker where I planned to give Grace her first bottle each morning. As I would later learn, "Don't ask, don't tell" is more or less the national motto in China. I got into the spirit early by deciding I'd say nothing unless asked directly, "Is there a rodent under that chair?"

Nothing left but to write the $18,000 check, which included everything from translations to travel, as well as the mandatory orphanage "donation" of $3,000. I can honestly say that I gave not one moment's thought to the legality of the process, though I've given it plenty of thought since. There was, of course, a fundamental immorality at the root of it all. In the best of all possible worlds, Chinese parents would be raising their own infants in their own homes. But I knew it was a Malthusian fact of Chinese life that the over-populated country could not, in fact, support all its babies. It seemed sensible to me that China should have tried to limit its population. And it seemed (and seems) sensible to me that when babies who could not be fed were born anyway, they should be raised by anyone who could afford to do so: Chinese, preferably; foreign, if necessary.

For at the time, China was viewed as by far the least dodgy source of an international adoption. Other countries' adoption programs had been scarred by scandal, but China was known for an aboveboard process governed by government-to-government protocols, not by supply and demand in some foreign alleyway.

The role of the US government in the process—US parents had to get approval from the federal government before Beijing would allow them to adopt—gave me the moral cover I was looking for. China's adoption program would later be tarnished by revelations that traffickers bought babies and sold them to some orphanages for international adoption. But back in 1999, when I was preparing my dossier, I heard not a whiff of such practices, and I do not believe they were widespread at the time. Many of us chose China precisely because we considered it the most legitimate. It had everything to do with availability and nothing to do with ethnicity.

I'd just come up from the cellar after doing my morning rounds of the spring-loaded traps that broke the necks of my rodent invaders. Wearing thick yellow dishwashing gloves, I emptied the traps into the trash can in the alley-way after steeling myself for the teeming mass of baby rats that were usually nesting near the top of the bin. I tossed in my kill, wondering whether I'd have to do this with a baby on my back in the very near future. And before I got the gloves off and the kettle on for my first cup of tea, the phone was ringing.

"Her name is Yang Shu Min, and she's from the best orphanage in China. You are very lucky," said the sweet reedy voice of Junji Chen, the best news I had ever heard by a long shot. I rushed out, leaving an egg boiling black on the stove, hurtling down the street, a middle-aged woman clad in sweat suit, panic, and boundless joy. Ms. Chen had a courier package from China that would make me a mother in an instant, without the labor pains. And soon she was handing me a little thumbnail photo against the red Chinese background, complete with tiny holes from the straight pin that had bound it to the paper-work that made us a family.

Yang Shu Min had me at the slightly furrowed brow. I vowed that no daughter of mine would ever look so worried again. From the shaved head to the wide-set eyes to the protruding ears, this was my kid. I had to name her on the spot: Grace (my mother's middle name), Shu Min (her Chinese name), and Waldmeir (nothing to be done about that.) I don't remember even notic-ing that she looked a bit Asian.

I rushed off to commandeer the copy machine at the local CVS to repro-duce that tiny photo in every conceivable shape and size, a virtual baby to hold the spot for the real one. There was a photo in the crib, one in the highchair, and another in the rocker, above the glue-trapped rat. And there was even a virtual Grace in the empty car seat as I drove around town, buying everything I would need to make her happy.

Every night, I clutched that picture to my breast and wept for the mir-acle that was Grace. I howled for the bitter-spinster future that had been so narrowly averted; I gave thanks to the fates that sent me a child at just the moment when I knew I could no longer possibly live without one. And I sobbed for the sheer delight of being historically in the right place at the right time. Had I waited even a year, I would still be childless.

Six weeks later, a friend and I were hurtling through the Shanghai railway station, chasing a gnarled old crone who had improbably manhandled all nine of our bags onto a single handcart, which she was using as a battering ram against the teeming railway masses. We were about to miss the train to the eastern Chinese city of Nanjing, capital of Jiangsu province, where I was to pick up Yang Shu Min and make her Grace Shu Min Waldmeir. The pink paper tickets were in my hand, but the information on them might as well have been hieroglyphics: not a word of English anywhere. Not the destination name. Not the station name. Not the date or time or seat or car number. We were late because we couldn't read the tickets and had gone to the wrong railway station.

How could I miss the train that would take me to the biggest meeting of my life? For decades I'd waited, and my baby was due to arrive almost on the date of my forty-fifth birthday. But if we were late, I was sure they would give her to someone else.

Not if our old crone had anything to do with it. She all but leaped the ticket barrier, handing us on to a succession of other wiry touts, who eventually managed to insinuate us onto the train at the last moment. By the time I'd strewn copious handfuls of crumpled renminbi notes in their direction, abandoned half my luggage in the aisle and slumped, sweat soaked, into my plush upholstered seat, I'd lost whatever fragile grasp I still had on sanity. Bemused commuters were treated to the spectacle of a middle-aged white lady melting into a damp puddle surrounded by nine oversize pieces of luggage. Several asked my travel mate Julia Bucknall—who had kindly volunteered to use up her frequent-flier miles flying to China with me on The Race for Grace—whether I was ill. She mercifully lacked the Mandarin to say, "Only mentally."

Within hours, we'd checked into Nanjing's Central Hotel, with its dirty rug, cheap fittings, and chipped veneer furniture an impossibly mundane setting for this most miraculous of meetings. I unpacked those nine bags to build a veritable shrine to my new daughter. It was like a love note from Babies 'R Us to the child I could not yet even imagine: pacifiers in every available color, shape and size, just in case this child, who had never had anything to call her own in the orphanage, should prove to be finicky about pacifier shape; tubes and jars and bottles and packages of medicine, to treat everything from scabies to diaper rash; a bulbous syringe in baby blue, to clear mucus from her flat little nose; one tall narrow baby bottle and several squat ones, complete with every conceivable shape of nipple; an inflatable baby bath, in case she didn't like the hotel tub; a package of soy formula, in case she didn't like cow's milk; and baby rice cereal, in case China didn't have enough for her.

I had all the paraphernalia of perfect parenthood, but I was terrified. It was no small thing, after decades of single, professional, globe-trotting life, to sign over one's entire future to an unknown foundling who might be ill or disabled. At the very least, I knew she would require around-the-clock utter devotion, coupled with an ability to distinguish between cough and meningitis in the middle of the night when it would be just the two of us. No husband, no nanny, no experienced mother to help out. Just me and Yang Shu Min. Forever.

And then she was there, nearly an hour early. The kettle wasn't boiled for her first bottle; the formula had not been measured out, nor had the right nipple been chosen from the shrine in the corner. I was in the bath; I wasn't even dressed.

Julia opened the door, but she wasn't signing for any baby deliveries. So, to avoid confusing Yang Shu Min about who was Mommy, she slammed the door in her face. Mercifully aware that adopted baby deliveries can cause some strange behavior in foreigners, orphanage deputy director Lily Li cooled her heels in the hall, clutching my baby. Julia roused me from the bath and went to hide behind a chair in the corner. She wanted to give me privacy for the most astonishing experience of my life: the first time I held my first child—our first instant as a family.

Patti and Grace become a family

She couldn't bear to look me in my two round eyes. I'd waited a lifetime to be a mother, and my child could not stand the sight of me.

Her almond eyes were frantic, and she strong-armed me with all her infant might, arching away from the embrace that I had waited forever to give her. Eight-month-old Yang Shu Min had survived being left by the side of the road in the middle of a Chinese winter, the raw stump of umbilical cord garish against her newborn skin. She had endured the bone-damp chill, sweat-choked heat, and the benign neglect of a Chinese orphanage. And she had learned to forget the breast of the birth mother who suckled her, making do with a naked bottle thrust through the bars of her orphanage crib to suckle alone. She had taken all that in her stride. But being handed over to me—a bottle blonde with a big nose, round eyes, and skin of a color she had never seen before—appeared to have unnerved her. My beautiful new daughter whimpered once and was silent.

I was conscious of treating Yang Shu Min like a young wild animal: no sudden movements, no eye contact, no hostile gestures. Cradling her bristly shaved head tentatively against my cheek, I whispered nonthreatening nothings to her, susurrating sounds meant to promise what parents always promise: "It'll be OK, honey." By which I presumably meant that being ripped from the culture and nationality and language and lineage of her birth to grow up seven thousand miles away in a foreign country was going to work out just fine for her. It was pretty clear how all that was going down with Yang Shu Min, though; she was just barely tolerating me. Given the choice, I have no doubt she'd have opted for the orphanage.

In the five-odd minutes we'd been a family, the expression on her oval face had cycled through shock to wretchedness to simple surrender. I wanted to say, "I will always love you. I will never leave you. We will be happy together," but there would be plenty of time for that once that kettle boiled. I decided the cure for her infant angst was a warm bottle, a new toy, and a baby biscuit. I might have been foreign, but I mixed a mean Enfamil. I hoped upon hope that these signs of the good life to come, would overcome her culture shock.

But Yang Shu Min never got that first bottle because the Chinese government needed us right then to sign a few forms to make us forever a family.

This took a while, and through all of it, the only position my new daughter would tolerate was on my lap, facing outward toward a world that still, reassuringly, looked overwhelmingly Chinese. I could not cuddle her, breast to breast, for fear she would catch a glimpse of me and startle; I could not gaze reverently into her almond-shaped black eyes; I could not admire her. Put simply, I was white and, she was not. It had never occurred to me that she would notice.

Some of her pain I had expected; what infant likes strangers? What baby wants to see the sole familiar face in her firmament—in this case, the round-faced, gaudy-polyester-clad Ms. Li—hand her over and walk away? I'd expected Yang Shu Min to squirm and squall and maybe even go catatonic; other babies adopted from China had done the same or worse. But what I wasn't prepared for, from that very first glance between us, was the culture shock.

"Was that when I pooped on you?"

Yang Shu Min had heard the story of the handover scores of times, but for her, the undisputed highlight of the tale was always the fact that her first official act was to defecate on me.

It was supposed to be a moment of priceless bonding, the first bottle of our new life together. But Julia's hands were shaking so badly she could not open the package of formula, and neither of us could figure out the directions, which were in Chinese. We switched nipples a few times, fussed with a pillow to support the baby's head, and still Grace Shu Min wouldn't take the bottle. Starvation was imminent! And if she didn't eat, she wouldn't grow, and the Chinese government would repossess her from her incompetent mother. To this day, it's desperately easy to trip my "I am a bad mother" switch; back then, it was switched on all the time.

So I was mightily relieved when we finally found the right combination of nipple, bottle, formula, and water temperature, and Grace took her ceremonial first suck. That's when I noticed that my arms, leg, and the white hotel pillow were streaked with chartreuse. There was baby poop on everything, including the red, white, and blue Fourth of July dress that was Grace's special handover outfit, right down to tiny little American flag–embossed crew socks. Julia dubbed it Grace's First Crap, and mercifully, it sent us both into peals of laughter. That's what happens when you give an American-size bottle to a baby diapered a la Chinois; the flimsy Chinese diaper can't handle the American portion size. It was culture clash of the most elemental variety.

I was slumped against one of the red-and-gold tartan-covered hotel twin beds, wondering if it was time for Yang Shu Min's nap yet. She was cruising: stumbling from bed to bed, from me to Julia, tripping over rattles and blocks and electronic gadgets, savoring the one thing orphanage life could not give her—the freedom to wander.

It was a couple of days after the handover, and my baby had already taught herself how to crawl. Life in an institution was confined to crib and walker, so crawling was a skill she'd never seen the need for. But put a television remote control within eyeshot, and she'd summon herself onto all fours and collapse face first any number of times until she got to it.

After that first bottle, the first evacuation, and the first few hours of utter terror were out of the way, I began to get to know the new Grace Shu Min Waldmeir. Her name was a cultural dog's breakfast, but the kid herself emerged as purebred American by temperament long before she had the actual passport to prove it.

Sure, she hadn't seemed too keen on the sight of American faces in the early days, though she soon got used to us. But never was a child born with a more American temperament. Brash, self-confident, in your face, daunted by nothing—within days that was the Grace who began to emerge. She could not walk unaided—but she never met a wall she didn't want to climb. When she toddled into a room, she possessed it.

The orphanage staff had described her on paper as active, quick to smile, and having an anus of the dimensions 1.5 centimeters by 1.5 centimeters. I assumed none of that was to be taken too seriously. But the "active" part was, if anything, an understatement. After the first day or so, Grace and I never caught our breath. She perambulated ceaselessly through government offices, banquet restaurants, airplane aisles, and hotel lobbies, clutching my two fingers since she could not yet walk without them, never letting me sit down, take a bite of dinner, or even ease my cricked back. Maybe there's no word for *hyperactive* in Mandarin.

It was so much better than giving birth. I got a baby who already knew how to sleep through the night. (There weren't enough nannies to cuddle babies back to sleep, so orphanage infants quickly learned how to do it themselves.) She could sit up, pull herself to standing, and practically find the right buttons on the TV remote control. She was much more fun than a newborn.

Her ears stuck out almost at right angles from her shaved head (the orphanage usually shaved babies in summer to avoid heat rash and lice), and her eight-month-old body was lean and wiry and the size of an smaller-than-average six-month-old. Despite the bottomless selection of frilly frocked numbers that I dressed her in, she was often mistaken for a boy. Her back was covered with deep purple splotches, which I mercifully already knew were a common Asian skin pigmentation called Mongolian blue spot and not the painful bruises they appeared to be. And she got hysterical about things like diaper changes, putting on pajamas, and, heaven forbid, bathing. We eventually gave up trying to bathe her, even in the nifty inflatable baby bath. Instead, I'd just climb in the tub naked with Grace clasped tight against my chest and hope that Julia couldn't glimpse too much of my salt-and-pepper pubic hair while pouring water over both us.

Two days later, Grace was doing that strong-arm thing again. But this time, it wasn't me she was frantic to escape; it was Lily Li from the orphanage. In the time since Ms. Li had handed her over, Grace and I had become inseparable. I couldn't even put her down to go to the bathroom. Like many Chinese foundlings, she hadn't taken long to change sides and throw in her lot with us foreign devils. She was in no mood to go backward, not even into the arms of the kindhearted and ethnically familiar Ms. Li.

We were back where this all began: at the Yangzhou orphanage, home to Yang Shu Min for nearly all her first eight months. But what a difference forty-eight hours makes. No sign of recognition from her, of the place or of its people.

Hunger doubtless played a part in the crisis. We'd rousted the sleeping babies out of their cribs at 7:00 a.m. that day and bundled them into a bus for a three-hour journey to their putative hometown. So I was delighted when we were ushered straight off the bus into a sumptuous banquet and even more thrilled when the orphanage nannies took our bottles away to fill them with boiled water.

But when the nannies brought our bottles back, the water was scalding. I was just setting Grace's aside to cool when Ms. Li decided she could calm my baby. But she hadn't met the new Yang Shu Min, complete with American appetite. By then Grace had figured out that mealtime with the foreigners was nothing like feeding time at the orphanage. The trough was bottomless.

In those early days, the sight of food—or even an empty plate and chopsticks—could trigger in Grace what Julia called "the Ethiopian famine victim" response. I had to keep her strapped into her stroller whenever the promise of food was at hand; otherwise she would hurl herself at the table, trying to get at it. I took to feeding her three bowls of baby rice cereal and a couple of jars of baby food before we even set out for a meal, just to hold her over. And I never went out without the small slip of paper on which our Chinese guide had written "My baby needs steamed egg with rice." I never knew when she might have a hunger emergency.

As we sat at the loaded banquet table in the orphanage that underfed her, she became apoplectic at the sight of a bottle she couldn't suckle. Grace was so distraught that by the time the bottles were cool enough to drink, she wasn't calm enough to suck one. The nannies took her bottle away and gashed its nipple with a knife to make the hole bigger. But that just ensured that every time I tipped the bottle in her direction, her little seersucker smock—the one that her new Grandma Marilyn, my stepmother, had picked out specially for that day—got doused with sticky infant formula. By the time the others had finished their feast, Grace and I were slumped in a corner, exhausted. We let them go off to explore the orphanage without us.

I was glad for the excuse not to go along. I was in China under dubious pretenses; journalists were banned from Chinese adoption, and I was exactly the kind of foreign correspondent that Beijing least wanted snooping around the inside a Chinese orphanage with a video camera.

Terror of losing Grace dogged my every moment back then. Not the usual did-I-stab-the-baby-with-that-diaper-pin kind of anxiety. Not even the is-she-still-breathing variety that would hit me later, when I took to poking Grace in the wee hours just to make sure she was still alive. This was much more primal: I was terrified that Grace would be repossessed. So when the others went off to snap a few priceless photos of how our babies lived back then, I strapped Grace into a sling across my sweaty chest and hid.

I'd caught a glimpse on the way in, in any case. Nothing too Dickensian. It looked more like a three-star Chinese hotel, complete with ornate flocked wallpaper and giant banquet tables draped in red linen. Sure, the exterior walls were streaked with mold, and the squat toilets were dark and dank. But I'd seen far worse. In fact, when we passed through the ceremonial front gate, I burst into tears, proclaiming weepily, "But it's such a *nice* place."

The orphanage staff was certainly doing its best to make sure we were impressed. They'd been through all this before, enough times to know that happy adoptive parents make generous (and undiscriminating) donors. But the director was furious when he found the rest of our party wandering around the baby wing. That made me even more determined to get back on the bus.

Eventually, in the mysterious way that such things happen in China, the clandestine visit to the baby wing became an official authorized visit to the baby wing, and I got enough of a peek to register a few mental snapshots: infants lying crosswise, two to a crib, in a room devoid of any visible decoration; toddlers at the end of a hallway, each in her own well-used baby walker; and a hurried embrace from a middle-aged woman with a kind smile and badly permed hair, who claimed to be Grace's "special" caregiver, though Grace showed not a glimmer of recognition when the woman tried to hold her. Not nearly as bad as it could have been.

"I want you to know how grateful we all are for what a wonderful job you did raising our babies." I took it upon myself to suck up to the orphanage director before we were on our way. He replied, tetchily, that they had done their best but that China was a third world country. I bit my tongue before I could point out the obvious—that third world-orphanages don't really need sumptuous banquet wings—and it was a truce. Since Grace chose that moment to soil her diaper, forcing me to whip out the square of flannel-backed plastic that I carried around as a changing mat and wipe her bottom in full view of the director, China still had the last laugh that day. I could see the director thinking financial editors were not really all that good at changing diapers.

CHAPTER 5

Orphanage Sisters

BUT GRACE WASN'T THE ONLY Yang delivered that day; there were also four others. Left to right in their first group photo were Yang Xue, Yang Yunong, Yang Yuyao, Yang Shu Min, and Yang Yilin: all eight months old, all Chinese, all adopted on the same day in the same joint ceremony, so like sisters they even shared the same last name. Before they went off to start their new lives as Maya, Emma, Lily, Grace, and Natalie, we propped them up against a wall for the group photo that captured their kinship for a lifetime.

All five sets of parents, relatives, and friends were wielding multiple devices to record the moment. I was pretending to ignore the fact that Grace was so much more physically advanced than the others. She wouldn't sit still, while others couldn't even sit up. I was ashamed to be glad I got the super achiever. But that seemed to be how everyone felt: that they got the perfect baby.

Grace punched Natalie in the jaw, and then Nat biffed her back. Emma tumbled helplessly in the fray, unable to right herself, and shrieked in outrage at Maya, who seemed bemused at what she could possibly have done to offend her. Lily gazed off into the middle distance, above the melee. Their clothes proclaimed their new American identity—not least because none of them wore multiple layers of heavy clothing in the sweltering heat like every other baby in China, where baring too much infant skin, even in summer, is viewed as unhealthy. Our girls' limbs were free, and their knees were bare, just like the half-clothed American babies they would shortly become. But the bonds among them would not be severed by so small a thing as a change in clothing (or country).

Born within a fortnight of one another, all five spent their infancy together in the baby room of the orphanage in Yangzhou, the closest thing they had to a hometown. Grace and Emma shared a crib, and for the first few months of their lives, all of them shared the identical life story: wake at 5:30 a.m. to a bottle thrust through the bars of the crib, propped up on a folded cloth diaper if they could not hold it. Rice cereal and steamed egg dispensed by caregivers moving methodically down the row of cribs into tiny mouths turned upward for the nourishment. Two naps a day on command, diaper changes when the nannies had time, bottle before bedtime at 8:30 p.m., and up again at 5:30 a.m. No emotion, scant affection, not much special treatment. But a routine and a bed and a bottle they could count on. Theirs was reputed to be the best orphanage in China. Certainly, there were far worse ones.

The Yangzhou girls were as close to family as any of them might ever have in China. But that made the rest of us instantly a family, too. Five mothers, ranging in age from thirty-something to fifty-something, we all grabbed our babies and posed for our own adult version of the Yangzhou family photo. On one end was a middle-aged, impossibly youthful-looking me, wrestling to keep Grace on my lap. At the other end, the other single mother: thirty-something Nancy O'Brien, Washington lobbyist, with placid, smiley Maya. In between were thin, fit, and youthful stay-at-home mom Leslie Petro (Natalie); paving company heiress Tonia Mueller (Lily); and multinational executive Nancy Raff (Emma). In the back row were the husbands, for those who had them.

To say I had nothing in common with this unlikely crew of small businesspeople and farmers, restaurateurs and video game entrepreneurs, would be to overstate our degree of connection at that point. We had been thrown together entirely by happenstance. We all chose the same US adoption agency, which randomly chose to send our adoption paperwork to China at roughly the same time. We traveled as a group to keep down the costs of guides and ground transport, and Beijing obligingly picked a convenient group of five babies for our five families to adopt. We shared the most intimate ritual of a lifetime—becoming a family—before most of us had even met.

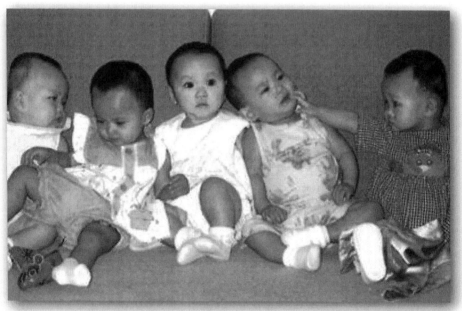

The Yangzhou girls: Maya, Emma, Lily, Grace and Natalie

I'd noticed one of the five families from the start: George and Leslie Petro. Handsome, dark haired, and trim, they already had two biological sons back home. Maybe that's why they seemed far saner than the rest of us. They proved to be the ones to tap if Julia and I wanted to try out a local specialty like duck tongue (which looks and tastes, unfortunately, like what it is). Time to check out the tiger paws, lizard skewers, and snake-flavored wine at the local market? George and Leslie were up for anything. They, almost alone among us, seemed to be enjoying China at least as much as having a new baby.

I hardly remember the other families: the sauerbraten-loving Mueller family; silent German Klaus and outspoken German American Tonia, who would come to be counted among my closest friends; Nancy O'Brien, the other single mother; or Nancy Raff, who lived in Paris, and Joe Distler, Emma's parents. Emma's mom gave me her business card during the trip, but I threw it away—that's how much I expected to remain in contact.

I had, if anything, even less interest in their babies, except to notice how inferior they were to mine. Natalie was so ill with a cold that she seldom emerged from the cave of George Petro's chest. Maya was always smiling, but her big head was so heavy that it kept tipping her over. Emma and Lily were self-contained and willing to stay mostly in one place. I wanted to bond with my daughter; I had no interest in bonding with the mothers and fathers and sisters and brothers of all her orphanage crib mates.

"How much do you earn?"

"Why do you want to adopt a baby from China?"

"Why don't you have children of your own?"

"Why aren't you married?"

We'd all had to answer all these questions in front of all the others as part of the process that formalized our adoptions. Just like a real family: no privacy. So though I had just met him, it was to George Petro, father of Natalie, that I turned in panic when the first of a series of Chinese officials asked me just about the most existential question imaginable: Why did I want to adopt a baby from China?

"Because China wanted to give me one" didn't seem the right reply. But George looked like the kind of guy who could charm his way past any cultural obstacle, so I turned to him for a better one. With pea-size Natalie curled up forlornly on his chest, he offered this: "I've always admired Chinese culture, and I plan to raise my daughter to admire it, too." I copied it verbatim.

Next, we had to get our fractious new charges to sit for passport photos. They would need to be declared Chinese by the Chinese state, via its passport office, before the US government could transform them into new Americans. And this was just the start of three solid days of meeting mostly bored Chinese officials to go through the motions of persuading them we were fit parents for their country's babies. And we did it all together, answering the most intimate of questions in front of the perfect strangers who had suddenly become our new best friends.

"Do you promise you will never abandon her?" Now that one had me speechless. It was our final interview with the local notary, the Chinese official who had the power to sign Yang Shu Min into my custody forever. And I couldn't speak for weeping. My nose was dripping, and I was squeezing Grace so hard she was squalling. And of course, every other member of the Yangzhou family was watching me and bawling, too, overcome by the sudden realization that this was all deadly serious stuff, this tragedy that had made us a family.

The notary was a kind man, and from his perch on a pleather sofa at the front of a cliché of a Chinese reception room—air-conditioned to frigidity and far too large for this most intimate of gatherings—he hastened to assure me, "We believe you, we believe you," so I would stop the waterworks. And he lifted a relieved Grace out of my arms to pose for the photo that made us, officially, a family. George Petro could be seen changing Natalie's diaper in the background. In those days, there was nothing we didn't do together.

By the time we were done, we had all sworn multiple times to various arms of the Chinese state to respect and honor the Chineseness of our children. But the man on the Chinese street seemed to think the girls were fortunate to be giving up their citizenship. "Lucky baby, lucky baby," the matrons and grandfathers of China would cluck as we perambulated, often as a group, through the midsummer streets of some of the mainland's hottest cities. I think we had all worried that ordinary Chinese might resent us for baby-snatching. Instead, we were repeatedly stopped by people who wanted to thank us. Those who had no English said it with their eyes. They seemed to think these children were lucky to be escaping a China that had not yet entered its boom years. When we landed in Guangzhou, a city in southern China where our babies would collect their US visas, there was spontaneous applause in the arrivals hall. China didn't have the self-esteem back then to realize that what was happening was a national calamity.

"She was deserted at the gate of the Donghu bathroom," said the official version of Yang Shu Min's life story. She and all her Yangzhou sisters shared a similar one. They were all abandoned at different spots and at slightly different ages; all were left to the mercy of a Yangzhou winter by parents who, for whatever reason, could not keep them.

Grace got to the orphanage on November 13, 1999, the date that she was left at a public bathhouse next to a police station in a suburb that was then on the outskirts of Yangzhou. The policemen took her to the orphanage, which named her. And so Yang Shu Min was born.

The orphanage staff—which by then was expert at guessing the age of abandoned newborns—looked at the state of her umbilical cord stump and other clues and assigned her an official birth date of November 7, 1999, six days earlier. No one knew when she was, in fact, born or where. Was it morning and rainy? Balmy and in a hospital? During a dark village night at home, attended by a traditional midwife? Was she her mother's first child or, more likely, the second, third, or even fourth? Did her parents already have a son or want one? Did they consider trying to hide her or give her to relatives to raise or, for that matter, sell her or worse? Did they try to scrape together the money to pay the excess-baby fine often levied under the one-child policy? Were they too poor to pay it, or did they prefer to spend the money on a new sofa? Or to save it for school fees for that eventual son? The orphanage paperwork didn't hazard any guesses. It just stated the obvious: "Yang Shu Min's natural parents and birthplace are not quite clear." All the Yangzhou girls' paperwork said something similar.

The police tried "by every means" to find her "own parents" but failed. So we were all told when orphanage staff presented us with grainy photocopies of the announcements that had been placed in a local newspaper. Grace's announcement informed her biological parents that they had sixty days to claim her—as though they had simply misplaced a six-day-old baby on the side of the road in wintertime. The announcement included line after line of similar notices, all for babies surnamed Yang, that included date of birth, putative finding place, and a couple of scant facial clues. Grace's said she was a "single eyelid" baby—that's the way Asians indicate whether a child has an eyelid with a fold (highly desirable) or without one (like Grace). It also stated that she had a high nasal arch. Nothing else.

So while Grace was supposedly waiting for her parents to come to their senses and welcome her back to hearth and home, she did her time at the Yangzhou Social Welfare Institute on the outskirts of town, a place that even most Yangzhou residents did not know was there. No records were kept of that period, apart from a handful of photos taken by orphanage staff with a disposable camera I sent them just before I arrived. They mostly showed a furrow-browed Grace doing things that we would later learn orphanage babies almost never did—like playing with toys while wearing pretty dresses, all donated by foreigners. Those were mostly only trotted out when officials visited or photos of happy children needed to be taken.

Eventually, after waiting the statutory period for her parents to turn up, Yang Shu Min's paperwork was sent, along with the documents of the other Yangzhou girls, to a place in Beijing that had an almost mythical status among adoptive parents: the "matching room" in the China Centre of Adoption Affairs. In that room, piled high with the files of countless desperate parents and anonymous orphans, a government bureaucrat somehow accomplished the miracle of matching me with Grace and her crib mates with their new parents, making all of us one giant extended family.

And about eight weeks from that moment when the Yang girls became Waldmeirs and Muellers and Petros and Distlers and O'Briens, we were all back in the United States after passing through a special line just for pint-size Chinese immigrants. And in their passports were American green cards that read "permission to work." Not only did we have new daughters, we had our own little breadwinners.

And still the Yangzhou family grew. Within a few short years, we were all back in China, adopting second daughters. None were from Yangzhou, but they fit right into the sisterhood formed on that day when we lined up Maya, Emma, Lily, Grace and Natalie against a wall and let them punch one another.

"The doctor would like to speak to you." No mother wants to hear such words. Almost as a formality, I had asked our pediatrician to review the medical record, complete with little red thumbnail photo, of Fu Xinke, the child Beijing had chosen to be my second daughter. I had expected him to compliment me on how cute she was.

Within a week of coming home with Grace, I had started the paper chase for a Chinese sister. Some eighteen months later, I was clutching the photo of a child about nine months old, whose face was so fat that she appeared to have no cheekbones or, for that matter, jaw. Another photo showed her baby limbs swaddled in so much padded cotton clothing that they stuck out stiffly at right angles. This wasn't a kid who looked unhealthy. But the doctor feared her liver was enlarged.

"It might just be a mistake," Grace's pediatrician said carefully, as I struggled to stop catastrophizing long enough actually to listen to what he was saying. I'd pulled my car into the local McDonald's, the same one whose drive-through I visited most mornings with Grace strapped in the car seat behind me to score a morning coffee without having to juggle both an active baby and a cup of hot liquid. The drive-through staff had recently started offering me a discounted "senior" coffee every morning, so motherhood had already aged me. How could I face the prospect of mothering not just an exhausting toddler but a critically ill infant to boot?

"If the medical report is correct, then it could mean a very serious or even fatal condition." It's strange discussing such life-or-death matters by phone while simultaneously watching others munch french fries. The doctor told me what the condition might be, but all I heard was "My baby is dying."

Biological parents may find it hard to credit, but in my mind, Fu Xinke—a child I had never seen, except in a tiny photo—was already my daughter.

I flipped shut my Nokia, sank dejectedly into the seat of a minivan that already had two car seats in it, and pondered my impossible options: adopt a possibly terminal ill child at great cost to my existing baby or refuse her on health grounds, knowing she would never be adopted. This is why God didn't make us all single parents, I thought. This kind of decision should not have to be made alone.

But when I got home, help was at hand. We had a Chinese lodger who hailed from Fu Xinke's home province; she pulled some strings. Little Xinke (nicknamed Keke by the orphanage staff) was given another medical exam, and presto, the enlarged liver disappeared. It turned out she was suffering not from a terminal illness but from poor Chinese record keeping.

"Can you teach me how to say 'I love you' in Chinese?" I asked our Chinese lodger. We were sitting at our dining room table with two wooden high chairs already pulled up to it, one with a grotesquely blown-up photo of Fu Xinke in it. The high chairs were retro, complete with antique spindles that I sanded and varnished myself. None of that easy-to-clean white plastic with bright vinyl padding like everyone else. Our house was strewn from finished basement to carpeted attic with plastic toys in every conceivable primary color, but I'd drawn the line at garish high chairs. Alone in our messy, toddler-centric house, the high chairs were tasteful.

"She won't know what you're saying," the lodger explained. I got a bit huffy, assuming she meant that with my tin ear, the kid would never get my drift. But that wasn't it. "Chinese parents never say that to their children," she explained. "My own mother never said that to me, either."

So this culture that could ask me with a straight face whether I planned to abandon a baby I had just traveled halfway across the world to adopt had no way to tell her I loved her? That seemed odd. Even on my brief trip to pick up Grace in China, I'd seen plenty of evidence that Chinese people adore babies—theirs and everyone else's. And no parent sacrifices more for her child than a Chinese tiger mom. How could anyone say Chinese people didn't love their kids?

But that's not what she meant. "Chinese parents show their love; they don't say it," she added, without drawing any unflattering parallels to how I was always cooing and blabbering sweet nothings to Grace. So I gave up trying to learn how to pronounce platitudes in Mandarin and focused instead on making sure I had enough loud electronic toys and defunct television remote controls for Fu Xinke to play with. It was time to build another shrine to American infanthood in another Chinese hotel room but this time, with far more toys and much less scabies cream.

Lucy's arms and legs were swathed in woolen long johns, and the sweltering heat had curled the wispy hairs at the nape of her plump baby neck. On the inside, she was dressed the way babies had been dressed in China for centuries: heavily, even on the hottest day. On the outside, she was decked out for a Fourth of July barbecue in the same skimpy sleeveless American flag dress her sister had worn for the handover, right down to the tiny flag-embossed socks.

The orphanage nannies clearly couldn't quite bear to dress her in the little summer outfit I'd sent for the handover, so they added a layer of thermals before launching her, unprotected, into a culture that didn't have the sense even to keep its babies warm.

But Lucy wasn't the type to be bothered by a spot of culture clash. She was just shy of her fourteen-month birthday, and I'd showed up early with a warm bottle, a package of teething biscuits, and her favorite toy drum to greet her. She was sitting up calmly on her own, on a metal folding chair in the unforgivably ugly city of Hefei, lighting up the room with her smiles. I'd brought bottle, biscuits, and toy as bribes to help her over her early jitters—except she didn't have any. When I reached out for her, she reached back. And when my long blond hair fell in her face, she amused herself yanking on it; the alien color didn't faze her.

This time, the notary just asked me, "You love the baby?" and I didn't even blubber. I was too busy urging my new daughter to walk to me across the dingy carpet, since it was clear she could already stand on her own. The oddly bloated photos that came with her paperwork had done nothing to prepare me for what I saw: a child who was stunningly beautiful, with big round eyes that shone with the joy of being alive in a way that only the really cutest toddlers can.

She obligingly waved a small American flag for those first precious photos, and we trotted off to find her some Sichuan scallops for our first meal together because I didn't want to raise a picky eater. Amazing how cavalier parents can get with that second one.

"Chinese people have a saying: Girls are like water splashing away; you spend money raising them, but when they marry, they join the husband's family, and their obligation is to care for his parents in old age—not you." We were jolting along the dusty rutted road to Lucy's orphanage, and our Chinese guide was broaching that most difficult of adoptive topics: Why throw away an infant girl just to try for a boy?

I'd left Lucy back at the hotel, which made it decidedly easier to focus on this potted sociology lesson. There was little to distract me in the way of scenery, that's for sure. Lucy's hometown was not like Yangzhou, with its graceful humpbacked bridges, ancient gardens, and imperial waterways. Chuzhou, Lucy's birthplace, was a gritty industrial city, still too poor to care what it looked like.

"She's probably the second or third daughter of a farmer," the guide speculated, referring to the complicated rules governing who could have how many babies under China's family-planning policy back then. Farmers could have two if the first was a girl, but if the second was a girl, too, their choices were limited: abandon the child, hide her with distant relatives, or try to get her secretly adopted by a friend or relative. Only those who could afford a fine that was three to ten times the annual income in some areas could keep a second or third daughter. The guide illustrated this talk with a visit to a local peasant home: no indoor toilet, night soil from the chamber pots used to fertilize the fields, a loom to weave straw into rope where the sofa would be back home.

On the way out of town, we made a brief stop at Lucy's putative place of abandonment. Her orphanage record said she was discovered at noon, weighed three kilograms, was forty-eight centimeters long, and had a temperature of 38.2 degrees Celsius "probably because of a chill." If true—and these records could be made up after the fact to satisfy adoption paperwork requirements—this gave a far more detailed picture of Lucy's earliest hours than anything I ever found out about Grace. But the bottom line was the same: "We tried hard to find her own parents for two months but failed. Fu Xinke is an abandoned baby definitely, and her own parents and her birth place are unknown," the paperwork concluded.

"When she sees me hugging other kids, she will cry sadly." This was written by Lucy's orphanage nanny, a round-faced middle-aged lady called Wang Houqing, when Keke was about nine months old. There was nothing remarkable about it, except the fact that anyone had thought to notice when Keke cried, let alone to write it down. None of the nannies at Grace's orphanage would have had the time or inclination to do so. But Keke was so bonded to Wang Houqing that she even knew what it felt like to be jealous.

I had the US charity Half the Sky Foundation to thank for that. It provided such nannies for thousands of Chinese orphanage babies. Since renamed OneSky, the charity provided a "hugging granny," or what her orphanage paperwork called a "designated grandmother," to play with Fu Xinke for a few hours every day, the hours that Grace would have spent lying in her crib or scooting around on her own in a walker. Keke's adoption paperwork indicated that granny Wang Houqing picked her up at 7:30 a.m. every day after a 5:30 a.m. breakfast of "rice gruel with formula, egg, sugar, and sometimes fruit or vegetable juice" and took her to play in the orphanage playroom, probably until lunch at 10:30 a.m. After napping from 11:00 a.m. to 1:00 p.m., Granny was back for the afternoon play session until snack time at 3:00 p.m. and dinner at 4:30 p.m. Or so I was told, along with other tidbits like the fact that Keke was "very lovely and adorable," "mutters to herself while playing music," and "urinates twelve times daily."

Wang Houqing took a photo of Lucy at about three months (an earlier photo than any I have of Grace) and penned two progress reports between winter and spring 2002, just before I got her. In them, Ms. Wang went on at length about how "smart and lovely" Keke was and bragged about how much she could eat. Maybe there was someone counting the bottles that Yang Shu Min could down in one sitting, but if so, they never told me.

Lucy was outraged. I'd explained many things to her during our two blissfully solitary weeks together in China, taking long walks and long naps and spending long days together just playing. But I'd forgotten to mention she had a sister. Lucy Waldmeir, age one, had just confronted Grace Waldmeir, age two, for the first time. Neither was pleased.

I could see why Lucy thought she was an only child, but I'd spent months preparing Grace for the arrival of a little sister, so it didn't seem reasonable for her to be acting so shocked. I'd read her book after book with titles like *I'm Going to be a Big Sister!* and *Little Rabbit's New Baby.* Sure, they portrayed the new arrival as a little slip of a thing swaddled in a blanket, not a solidly built toddler who'd already learned to give as good as she got. But Grace couldn't say I didn't warn her.

I'd often told her a version of her own adoption story; I even recorded it on a cassette tape to be played to her at bedtime while I was in China collecting Lucy. It went like this: "Once upon a time, a very beautiful baby was born in China, and her name was Yang Shu Min. Everybody wanted to be Shu Min's Mommy, everybody! But only this Mommy was chosen to be Shu Min's Mommy, and she was so happy, she cried with joy. She got on one airplane, and another airplane, and another airplane, and a train and a car and a boat and a bus and a taxi to take her to her baby girl. And when she held Shu Min in her arms, she said, 'You are my baby girl. You will always be my baby girl. I will always love you.'" But I never got to the end of that saccharine love song without Grace insisting that I jump straight to the poop part. And since some of her friends' mothers were having babies around then, too, she asked for further clarification on how the umbilical cord part worked in an adoption. I said it was more like a telephone line. "But how did you know my phone number?" she asked.

Lucy and I had just flown thousands of miles back from China, and I was as tired as if I had walked all the way, carrying her. It was nighttime for us, but a bright and cheery 7:00 a.m. for Grace, who had just awakened full of her usual manic energy. Somehow, I had to manage two warring toddlers, at least until naptime.

The next few days were mercifully erased from my memory by a mixture of jet lag and stubborn refusal to admit I was crazy to adopt two babies on my own. But the family photo album doesn't lie: for every sweet photo of the two toddlers wedged into the same high chair at mealtime, or tumbled together asleep in the same crib, there's one of Grace jamming a bottle angrily into Lucy's face, or dumping a bowl of soup over her head. Photo after photo shows the two girls side by side in their double stroller, in their twin car seats, and in those tasteful high chairs. But it's quite clear they were just barely tolerating the togetherness. My favorite was a photo taken within hours of that first meeting, which I sent out as an adoption announcement: the two girls sweaty and naked, slumped side by side in twin baby swings on the swing set behind our house. They looked exhausted.

"Are they twins?" If I had a dollar for every time someone asked me that when Grace and Lucy were kids, I'd already have funded their college accounts. It didn't help that I almost always dressed them in matching outfits—a practice that, before and since, I have considered tasteless but seemed an unaccountably good idea at the time. And then, of course, there's the fact that they were both Chinese.

But it wasn't just a case of Americans thinking all Asians look alike; even Chinese people in America would ask if they were twins. One was about a head taller than the other, and one had round eyes and the other almond ones, but there was, and is, something of the sibling about them. We certainly were all well suited to one another. Both girls were sturdy, fearless, adventuresome, indestructible, and had boundless reserves of energy. Both tended to the hyperactive, which is lucky since I was a bit hyperactive, too.

Our backyard was set up like an adventure playground, with permanent paddling pool complete with plastic inflatable palm tree, jungle gym, water slide, molded plastic play kitchens, play cars, and playhouses dotted around so densely that our backyard grass never recovered. And if we got bored there—which we often did—we could be found at the zoo or the pool or the splash park. And every other Friday, we could be found at the local nature center watching the ranger feed a live mouse to the boa constrictor. And that's when we weren't on a road trip of East Coast amusement parks. When we drove to visit my family in Detroit, we'd hit every roller coaster along the way. My neighbor and their honorary godmother, my dear friend Stefanie Taylor, thought we should maybe spend a bit more time at home. But the truth is I was never very good at playing with toddlers. I needed more stimulation. I probably also needed the adult company. I had five months of maternity leave with each child, nearly back to back. That proved a long time to talk only to toddlers.

And doubtless I also liked the limelight. A middle-aged woman pushing fifty pounds of toddler around in a double stroller is going to attract attention at the best of times, but if they are both Chinese and obviously adopted? That attracts something more like adulation. Random strangers in the grocery store were wont to launch into paeans of praise. Obviously, no one would have thought to eulogize me like that if I'd suffered nine months of gestation with each one; that would have been considered unremarkable. But write a check for a few thousand dollars apiece and hop a plane to China, and you're virtually awarded the Nobel Peace Prize.

Nobody really got it. I adopted them for me, not for them. I wasn't saving little girls from evil Chinese boy preference or the one-child policy or communism or whatever narrative Americans sometimes spun around adoption. I wanted me some babies. And I got the best ones on earth.

Every year on their birthdays, I wrote a letter to each of them, trying to capture those things about them that the camera didn't record and my feeble memory could not retain. Those letters record that, within weeks of our return from China, both girls had settled so comfortably into their roles of big and little sister that Grace would often turn to me and say, "Mom, isn't Lucy cute?" And Lucy would obligingly play the baby of the family, though this wasn't a role that came naturally to her super-competent, over-responsible nature. Soon I had two babies so filled with the joy of living that I often wondered what they fed them at that orphanage.

And lucky for them, they had not just my own extended family to love them—and they did, before we even knew their names—but the Yangzhou family, too. Soon after Lucy and I returned from China, we lined up as many of the Yangzhou girls as we could muster (Emma was living in Paris by then, but the others came in from Illinois and Virginia and Western

Maryland for Lucy's homecoming) and snapped a group photo just like that first one when the Yangzhou girls were babes. And over the top of the sofa on which the older girls were perched, Lucy poked her tousled head. Accidental Americans, living in the accidental families that Beijing built. Thank God for accidents.

CHAPTER 6

We Are All One Family

WE WERE BACK AT THE same Shanghai railway station where the Race for Grace began, laden with bags of blueberry, cucumber, and hot-and-sour-fish-soup flavored potato chips for the journey, rather than Pampers and scabies ointment.

We had just moved to China the month before, and I figured there was no better way to mark the beginning of our root-seeking journey than to return to where it all began, in the baby rooms where the Yangzhou girls spent their infancy. And we'd be there in time for the eighth anniversary of Grace's Gotcha Day, the day we became a family—the first time Grace would celebrate that milestone without her orphanage sisters.

As usual, she only had eyes for the chips and the Oreos and the *fangbianmian*, literally "convenient noodles" or cup noodles, that we had laid in for the five-hour trip. A pilgrimage back to the orphanage was almost a staple of Chinese adoptive family life by then. Plenty had gone before us and reported back favorably that a huge fuss was made over the returning daughters. I'd consulted earlier pilgrims about how to prepare both my daughters, then aged seven and eight, for the visit.

So I settled them in two padded seats right next to an aromatic train toilet and tipped boiling water into the sturdy cardboard containers that the noodles came in. Back home, cup noodles had been verboten for all the salt, sugar, and other unmentionables that made them both so unhealthy and so utterly irresistible. But I wanted to induce a positive state of mind for a chat about homecoming, and back then, the best way to their attention spans was always through their taste buds.

Luckily, the savory smell of the spicy beef brisket–flavored noodles over-powered the toilet stench. The girls bent their heads down close over the rim and peered through the steam to watch a nearby passenger hold her baby over a trash can and aim his tiny penis through his split pants so that he could pee into it. That was a treat they didn't often get in America, either.

"How do you feel about going back to the orphanage, Grace?" I asked, wishing I could think of a subtler way to tease out her emotions.

"Uh…fine," she slurped between mouthfuls of slippery delight. She'd been looking at our few treasured photos of her life at Yangzhou for as long as she could remember. They were bound in our most precious photo album, the one with the delicately hand-drawn calligraphy cover made by her kindergar-ten teacher at Rockville Chinese School.

The message was—or at least I hoped it was—that her life in China was a cherished part of her story. Not something to fear, not something to forget, and definitely not something to be ashamed of. Like so much about adoption, it just "was." Most of her closest friends had an identical story; theirs seemed as normal to them as grainy fetus scans and delivery room pics seemed to their blonder classmates back home.

I pondered whether there wasn't something more profoundly maternal I could say at that point to prepare her for the experience ahead. But she already had one hand in the package of raspberry-flavored Oreos and a thumb poised over Super Mario, so I figured the meaningful chat might have to wait until later.

I was banking on treats to carry her through: first the noodles, then the luxury hotel I had booked in Yangzhou, with as many visits to the local McDonald's and trips to the arcade as her heart could possibly desire. From the start, this was always my strategy to help them learn to love their home-land: bribe them.

Spending too much on hotel rooms was another part of my strategy. In Yangzhou, I had chosen the most expensive one available, at a hundred dollars a night. It wasn't hard to impress Grace and Lucy back then; they were still into pushing elevator buttons for fun. But they were thrilled even so. Room 8306 at the Yangzhou State Guest House, formerly the preserve of visiting

Communist Party dignitaries, had a glass wall between the slick marble bathroom and the California king–size bed covered in silks and satins (or at least polyester imitations of them). Pagodas outlined at night with fairy lights were dotted around grounds fit for an emperor or a Communist dictator. And the bathroom boasted plenty of lurid packages with suggestive labels to make the children giggle.

Every night, an invisible servant placed a "pillow menu" on our rock-hard bed: "The person has from cradle to the grave 1/3 times spend in the sleep, the pillow can be treated as concomitant the most long of time colleague," it opined, in the kind of English common in China at the time. To think I'd reached the age of fifty-three by then without ever having learned the Chinglish for *concomitant.*

But the hands-down best thing about the Yangzhou State Guest House from native daughter Yang Shu Min's point of view was the chocolate fountain. For a child born of a culture that doesn't generally much like sweets, Grace Shu Min Waldmeir was crazy about them. And none more so than chocolate, preferably cascading down from a great height in a cloying waterfall of sweetness.

Her cheeks streaked brown and her tummy feeling happy with China, Grace adjourned to our palatial room to wish the other Yangzhou girls many happy returns of their adoption day by phone. One was away at camp, and another had the answering machine on, but Grace spoke to Lily Mueller. "Guess where I am?" Grace asked, standing up on the bed to peer out at the vision of humpbacked bridges and ornamental waterways outside, like a landscape architect's cliché of Chineseness. Then she rushed to answer her own question. "I'm where you and I were born!"

Even from across the room, I could hear Lily squeal, "No kidding!" Her mother later told me that Lily had stomped her foot in frustration when she found out that Grace had gotten back to Yangzhou before she had.

Grace was leaning over the edge of the crib, dressed in her favorite washed-out cotton dress with the gaudy peony print, the one that she picked out back home at Sears after she returned all the tasteful clothes Grandma had bought her. "Look, Mom, isn't she so cute?" She was mesmerized by the week-old baby lying fast asleep on the thin bamboo mat within.

The nameless infant had just arrived at the orphanage, brought in off the street where desperate parents had left her, at the same age and in the same state as Grace eight years before. The parallel wasn't lost on my daughter. "Wow, Mom, this baby is exactly as old as I was!" she exclaimed. Grace was in a big "Wow, Mom" phase back then, her personality a beguiling mix of adult sensitivity and childlike wonder. Her face lit up with obvious delight at the thought that this placid infant, swaddled tight in a cozy orphanage blanket, had a life story that so paralleled her own. That might seem an odd thing to thrill an eight-year-old, but not that eight-year-old. It was easy to see her imagining herself at the start, her eyelids lightly shut and her face relaxed in sleep the way that only baby faces can be. It was as peaceful an image of her beginnings as I could have hoped for. Grace remembered that baby for years, but not with sadness—more as another little Yangzhou sister.

We'd spent half a day at the orphanage, the first time Grace had seen it since she was a babe in arms herself. I asked how it made her feel on a scale of happy to sad?

"Happy" she said, as I videoed the exchange. "It's nice to see the place where I was as a baby." She averted her gaze in shyness. Maybe she felt like she was supposed to say something different, but more likely, she just didn't like being videotaped at any time, not just when being grilled by Mom about something so personal.

The orphanage director treated us to a banquet of local delicacies— Yangzhou is home to one of the four great cuisines of China: *huaiyangcai*, the ancient food of emperors—though he laid in some of the hometown's famous Yangzhou fried rice for the kids, who picked out the shrimp but savored the carbs anyway. As Grace and Lucy played with the chopsticks and poured glass upon glass of Coke (a banned substance before we moved to China, but permitted as a useful bribe afterward), he filled me in on how adoptions from his institute had plummeted from 150 annually when Grace was born to only 15 a year by 2008.

Grace was mostly bored by all that, but she did want to know one thing: "Do some kids have to spend their whole lives here?" she asked carefully, not wanting to offend him. Even then, she had a natural exquisite politeness that she must have inherited from her birth parents, since I could never have given it to her.

The director was doing his best for babies like her, she later told me. She didn't want him to feel she was ungrateful. But she still breathed an audible sigh of relief when she heard that most healthy babies made it out by age one. Parents had even recently been found for some of the older and mildly handicapped kids. That was clearly the news she was waiting for.

But that meant the orphanage was filled with badly handicapped kids, and Grace squirmed at the sight of them. Abandonments of healthy infants like herself had all but stopped by then, and she wanted to know why. So did I; the journalist in me wanted answers. And so for the first time, I heard an explanation that I would later hear from orphanage officials all over China: prosperity meant more families could keep their babies, urbanization and mechanization meant they no longer needed male brawn to work the fields, and most of all, girls by then were just plain cheaper to raise than boys. Parents of sons had to send them to college and buy them a car and an apartment before anyone would marry them; daughters required much less and were nicer to have around in your dotage anyway. I knew it was a lot harder for foreigners to adopt from China by then; my own cousin had been waiting for years for a second Chinese baby. But I had no idea that what had happened in Yangzhou was happening all over China. The adoption window, open only oh, so briefly, was shutting; I couldn't believe the luck I'd had in striking the timing so right.

We bade the director farewell—but not before he asked me to buy the orphanage a loaded thousand-dollar laptop.

Grace at her finding spot

I was cross with Grace, and she was cross with me. Shoulders slumped, bottom lip stuck out for emphasis, she was grudgingly posing for a photograph on the spot where her parents had abandoned her. The place, originally a communal bathroom, had morphed in line with China's rise into a "leisure center." I was in tears at the vision in my mind's eye of baby Grace left in a rush basket or a cardboard box or a grocery bag on this spot, hard against the wall of the local police station.

Grace was unutterably bored by the whole thing and just wanted to move on to the outing (read bribe) I had planned next: letting her drive an electric boat through the canals of her hometown. She knew that this was "the place where you were found," as I'd carefully phrased it. (Its official title in the orphanage paperwork was her "place of abandonment,") She just couldn't have cared less. From the start, she had known this part of her story: that her parents couldn't keep her because it wasn't legal, so they put her some place safe where she would quickly be discovered and taken to live with me in America. She had zero interest in that actual place and even less tolerance for the fact that I was weeping over it. She simply could not grasp then, and would not for as long as I thought to ask her about it, why the place made me cry.

I eventually corralled her for a very bad-tempered photo, and then we promptly adjourned to see the sites of 2,500-year-old Yangzhou, one of the loveliest cities in China. She steered a boat around the inlets of the city's famous Slender West Lake without regard for bridge buttresses or our security deposit. Then we found an amusement park where the bumper cars crashed at velocities that would be considered human rights abuses in the United States and rode home in a motorized rickshaw with a driver who thought nothing of stopping dead when crossing a six-lane highway just to gawk at our unlikely family. As I often told the kids, where else would I let them risk their lives and call it a cultural experience?

The next day was lunch with Ms. Li, the lady who had put baby Grace in my arms eight years before. She'd made a special trip from the provincial capital just to see us, and she recalled that she'd been fond of Grace because she was so "gentle and quiet." (A case of mistaken identity, surely.)

And then over our hotel breakfast on the final day—where Yangzhou breakfast buns packed with chopped pork belly swimming in savory soup cozied up next to bacon and eggs—Grace told me her nightmare. "I dreamed that you were smoking cigarettes and died," she said. (This had happened to my own mother.) "Then all our other relatives died, and I was left alone to look after Lucy!" She looked both frightened and somehow embarrassed. I was mortified: Had returning to the orphanage marked her for life? But Grace said it was actually fun seeing what mischief she and Lucy could get up to in the dream without me there to cramp their style. Or that was her version at the time anyway. She may tell a therapist something altogether different one day when I am no longer around to defend myself.

We went back to Shanghai the next day, sad to be leaving a place so friendly and pretty, where people still had time chat and where I'd finally begun to discover a hint of the connection to China that we'd all moved there to cultivate. Yangzhou steamed buns—chicken soup for the tortured foreign soul—but also the kindness of the people of Yangzhou. That rickshaw driver who nearly got us killed on the way back to the hotel? Once he heard that Grace was born in Yangzhou, he could not have been more thrilled. "*Women shi yi jia ren,*" he said ("We are all one family"), patting her head and giving me a discount on the ride.

The Waldmeir family in Grace's hometown of Yangzhou

"What amount would you like the receipt to show?" Grace had had her hometown visit, and now it was time for Lucy to do the same. She was eight—the same age Grace had been when we visited Yangzhou—and we'd all taken a similar train, complete with similar cup noodles, to Lucy's birthplace of Chuzhou. But her homecoming was staged on an altogether more professional level, which is how the orphanage director got to asking me about the receipt.

His tobacco-stained teeth and oleaginous smile were vintage Chinese bureaucrat, but his shirt was Oxford blue, his tie would have been tasteful on Wall Street, and his bear hugs were the foreign kind, all showy and un-Chinese. We were sitting, with Lucy between us like a hostage, beneath a giant illuminated LED screen shrieking "WELCOME: Lucy Helen Xinke Waldmeir," in glowing gold letters against a background of pixelated Chinese red. We were the first foreign adoptive family to visit the institution's new reception hall, with its gilded ceiling and chandelier in the shape of Beijing's Olympic Water Cube in the town that was too poor to raise my baby.

Lucy's arms could barely make it around the bubblegum-pink bouquet of stuffed monkeys that her hometown had given her as a present. The portly, fatherly orphanage director was cuddling my little girl and pointedly calling her by her erstwhile orphanage nickname, Keke, knowing that adoptive families were prone to making large donations in exchange for creating fond memories for foundlings.

Chuzhou had her at the stuffed monkeys. Dolled up for the occasion in her favorite combination of chiffon party dress and beach sandals, Lucy cocked her head to the side just so and beamed for the paparazzi. She wasn't noticing the tense interchange we were having on the receipt issue.

I'd taken no cash to Chuzhou. "I'm very happy to buy a washing machine or a refrigerator for the orphanage. Let's go to the shop together and pick one out," I suggested.

But I wasn't getting away with the empty wallet excuse. "I'm afraid we've already used your donation to buy new quilts for the older children's beds, since it's nearly winter," he persisted.

"How much did they cost?" I asked, displaying the New World naivete so despised in the ancient culture that is China.

"Well, how much would you like to give?" he countered.

In the end, we went to the ATM, and I counted out twenty-five crisp red hundred-renminbi bills, knowing full well the bedding cost a fraction of that, and shushed Grace when she asked, "If they can afford a gold ceiling, why can't they afford quilts for the beds?" Reason not the need. Like others before me, I went to Lucy's hometown with my heart overflowing with gratitude for the priceless gift of my precious child. Chuzhou was just trying to relieve me of the uncomfortable burden of all that thankfulness.

"You were so beautiful when you were a baby, and you're still beautiful now. Just look at your long, long hair!" Lucy's designated grandmother, Wang Houqing, exclaimed, scooping her into a capacious embrace. Ms. Wang had the same wide, round, flat face as Lucy herself, the trademark physiognomy of their shared native province of Anhui. And she was indeed the closest thing to Lucy's granny, even if she had been paid to do that job by Half the Sky Foundation. Her job was not to feed Lucy or bathe her or wipe her bottom; she was paid just to play with her and a handful of other lucky Chuzhou babies: talk to them, stimulate them, and give them all a taste of what it was like to have someone who loved them.

On our return visit, the director waltzed with Lucy, serenaded her with ballads over lunch (during which he consumed most of the bottle of *baijiu* I had brought as a present for the entire staff), and managed to make sure every photograph showed him nuzzling her. But Wang Houqing choked up at the sight of Keke, in the way only a surrogate grandmother could do. She knew things about her that no one else could know. And she even seemed genuinely embarrassed when we presented her with an eighty-dollar Swarovski crystal miniature vase complete with tiny tulips as a gift.

But the truth is, Lucy was taken in by the whole performance anyway: by what I judged to be Wang Houqing's genuine emotion and what I judged to be artifice on the director's part. "My hugging granny was very, very, *very* happy to see me," she confided as we lay in bed after the visit. "My orphanage is much nicer than Grace's, don't you think, Mom?"

I wasn't taking that bait, but I had to admit, at least to myself, that I liked her dirty, poor, no-pretensions hometown at least as much as I liked Yangzhou, with its imperial pedigree. At Chuzhou, all the nannies called her by her baby name; at Yangzhou, none of the staff even knew whether Grace had one.

Everywhere we looked in Yangzhou, we saw fairy lights and ancient gardens; in Chuzhou, the roads were potholed, the lanes were dank, the huts were basic, and the dark skin of the peasant was everywhere. But we could not doubt the warmth of Chuzhou's welcome for Lucy as a lost daughter of Anhui. One man riding a bicycle by the side of the road nearly crashed into a tree for staring at us and grinning, and a taxi driver risked all our lives by repeatedly gazing back into the back seat to make sure he could believe his eyes; was there really a little Anhui girl back there speaking English? And everywhere we went, we were invited to sit a while and chat—something that never happened in Shanghai-on-steroids.

After three days of checking out everything from her (almost certainly fictitious) finding place—a completely different spot than the location I'd been taken to previously—to the sacred mountain that borders the town, Langyashan, where the girls spent hours fishing for translucent miniature shrimp in the mountain streams, I'd concluded that the visit would have been cheap at twice the price. To give Lucy warm and cuddly memories of her difficult start to life, I was prepared to pay any price. Call it therapy, with Chinese characteristics.

"Ya know, it's a bit much that when you go out just to buy a DVD, you have to see people with no arms, no legs, and no *face*," Lucy exploded. The twin orphanage pilgrimages seemed to have helped us all settle into our lives in China: good and bad. I'd given the kids five dollars to go down the road to the pirate DVD shop to buy us some flicks for family movie night, a ritual we enacted most Saturdays, while I relaxed over a cup of too-sweet Chinese coffee in the nearby bakery.

"Mom, we gave one *kuai* (fifteen cents) to a beggar, but we had to choose between the old guy and the guy with no legs," Lucy said, angry at being forced to make more such moral choices each day that a normal American child might face in a lifetime. She insisted I go back and give the legless fellow fifteen cents, too, and for once, I dispensed with the lecture about how begging is often organized crime in China, and the beggars don't actually get the money. Unlike the average American girl, Lucy was well aware of that, but she didn't want to step over that guy's prone form one more time without paying at least some price for it.

She differed from Grace in that way. Grace felt that China really had nothing to do with her. Asked once by a desperate Chinese passenger to translate from Chinese to English in the transit lounge of the Moscow airport, Grace said simply, "I'm not Chinese," leaving him mystified. Lucy seemed to take it all more to heart.

But they both hated many aspects of life there. "I don't plan to come back to China when I'm a grown-up," Lucy announced one day as we shoved our way onto the Shanghai subway at rush hour.

"Now, honey," I began, sensing a teachable moment to point out that Shanghai wasn't the only big city in the world whose public transit is a nightmare at rush hour. "In fact," I began to drone on, "it's cleaner, newer, and faster than public transport in London, New York, or Par—"

But she was not having it. "Pee, pooh, and stink," she cut me off to say. "The whole city smells, the toilets are disgusting, and taxi drivers pee on the side of the road. And on top of that, everyone *spits*," she said, hurling out that final insult. She made sure to point out every gob of spittle: "You see, that is spit, and this is spit, and that is spit, and that is more spit," she intoned. She was triumphant when she found a pool of spittle with blood in it. "The only thing that is better in China is the fireworks."

"Do you like living in Shanghai?" a consular officer at the US embassy asked her a few minutes later. (We had gone there to renew her passport.) Lucy looked at me helplessly. She was not a rude child.

"Tell him what we were just talking about," I suggested, meaning the bit about the fireworks.

"There's spit everywhere," Lucy said. At least she didn't mention the spit with the blood in it.

"Mom, am I black or white?" Lucy asked me at around that same time, as we cuddled up on family movie night to watch *The Help*, the movie about a black maid in the American South of the 1950s.

"Well, in South Africa, you'd have been classified as an honorary white under apartheid," I said, trying to buy time to come up with a way not to point out the obvious: that she is neither black nor white but a different shade altogether.

"I mean, could I have used the same toilet as you?" she asked. I didn't know the answer, but I knew that was the kind of question that propelled me to bring the girls to China in the first place.

CHAPTER 7

Learning to be Chinese in China

"Pee, pooh, and stink" was Lucy's snap verdict on her homeland. But over time—inexorably, imperceptibly, and to all of us—China began to seem like home. We all began to love it, first and foremost, through its food. Hearts and minds would take longer to conquer, but our bellies loved the place before we even got there. And even on the darkest days, all it took was one thin coin and the time to stroll down to any Chinese bun stall to cheer us all up with a cuisine that is so comforting, it's more like love.

The steam rising from teetering towers of bamboo advertised the delectable fare within: smooth white balls of yeasty dough, filled with slightly sweet and very oily leek and tofu or pork and cabbage or mystery fillings I never knew the name of. None of us knew what any of them were called, so we took potluck. But no matter what we ended up with, one dollar would buy us enough *baozi* happiness to make us feel happy all day.

At dawn, every other street corner would sprout vendors of traditional Shanghainese breakfast: mostly poor, mostly migrant cooks behind spitting griddles or vats of gruel or steaming towers of bamboo baskets, full of the fat, sweet, sometimes spicy food that Shanghai wanted for breakfast.

Our favorites were the soup-filled, crispy-bottomed *shengjianmantou* dispensed from a flat-bottomed skillet as wide as my arm was long. I loved being there when the cook turned off the gas, and the puffed-up tops of the buns dimpled as they sank down toward a meat filling laced with dollops of pork fat. A close second was *congyoubing*, or scallion pancakes, which came in every shape and size from thick to thin, from greasy to fluffy. (The kids preferred the floppy thin ones like a crepe.) Yeasty steamed *baozi* filled with sautéed greens and tofu were next on our list, followed by *zhou*, or rice gruel, packed with strips of pork and lumps of black and chartreuse thousand-year-old egg. I'd also been known to favor a crispy *jianbing* pancake filled with egg, garlic, scallion, and an extra dose of chili sauce, brushed with bean paste and wrapped around a deep fried strip of dough, just for the texture.

We never struggled to love China when our chins dripped grease from a *shengjianmantou* or the cook was spreading the *jianbing* dough paper thin on the hot griddle. Our stomachs were changed forever by those encounters. More than a decade later, Chinese food is still the only kind that really satisfies us; in fact, it's more like an addiction. Forced to make a choice, we'd take pot stickers with us to a desert island, not hamburgers. A corner of our foreign tummies would be forever China. There was still more work to do on our hearts and minds, though.

"I'm more Chinese than Grace," Lucy announced as I struggled to persuade them that the pork and crab *xiaolongbao* (traditional Shanghainese soup dumplings) would not really taste like seafood, and they tried to persuade me just to order another plate of *guotie*, or pot stickers.

Grace had a standing order at the dumpling place on the corner, and the owner knew what it was before we were halfway in the door: four plates of greasy *guotie*, hold the vegetables. Lucy always had gruel with thousand-year-old egg and a side of spinach stir-fried with garlic. And I always had the house soup dumplings and snuck in pork and crab when I could turn the bamboo tower away from them so that they couldn't see the word *crab* written in Chinese on the side of it.

Like many families, we talked best over food. "I'm good at Chinese sports like ping pong and badminton; I like Chinese food more than Grace does." (Lucy had taken, around then, to saying hamburgers were boring.) "And my style of dress is sort of Chinese, too, more girly," she said with a twirl of flounced pink miniskirt. Lucy even had the Chinese work ethic toward school; for several years running, I offered her a hundred renminbi (fifteen dollars) if she would get a B on her report card instead of all As.

"Grace is always trying so hard to prove she's not Chinese at all," Lucy concluded.

Grace concurred. "I'm a typical American. I have zits, and I like One Direction," Grace said proudly, referring to her obsession with the American boy band.

"You do realize that not everyone sees you the same way you see yourself?" I asked.

"I don't care," she said. "I don't like China. Sometimes I think you are more Chinese than I am." We went back to savoring the food that all of us could also agree on loving: Chinese dumplings. Even if Grace didn't want to share a nationality with them.

"Little girl, do you understand what I'm saying? This is very important!" Yet another taxi driver was trying to drive and deliver cultural pearls of wisdom to my children in the back seat in the strong, harsh tones of Shanghainese Mandarin. "Those people didn't take responsibility for you when you were a baby, and this foreigner did. There's no reason at all that you should look for them. They are bad people."

And just how exactly did we get onto the topic of Lucy's birth parents when all we wanted was a taxi ride to the mall for a bit of hot pot? Lucy was outraged when, as he let us off, he said, "Thank you": not for the fare but for raising one of the discarded daughters of China.

I didn't hear him, but Lucy did: "Mom! He said thank you. You should say something." She wasn't offended at the invasion of privacy. She was mad at Mom for being impolite.

Later, as she dipped razor-thin sliced pork and Napa cabbage into the steaming broth of our shared hot pot, she let off some steam of her own about the abandonment, which I had always tried to sugarcoat for her. The older my girls got, the more I tried to provide my best educated guess at what might have happened to them, but I always erred on the side of not blaming their parents, unlike the average taxi driver. "It's not like a Western adoption, where the parents have to give up the child voluntarily before it can be adopted." I'd said something along these lines so many times that it was almost rote by then. "Your birth parents almost certainly had no choice. Either they had too many other kids, and the government took you away, or maybe Grandma insisted they needed to try again for a boy. Either way, I don't think we can blame them for what happened."

But after that taxi ride, blame them Lucy did. "I wouldn't mind seeing a picture of them, just out of curiosity, but I don't care if I ever meet them," she said.

"But if you found them, don't you think you should spend some time with them at least" I inquired, pointing out that I'd interviewed a woman earlier that day who'd been threatened with a fine of three times her annual income for having an extra daughter.

But Lucy cut me off. She'd heard that one before, too. "I don't owe them anything. They wanted a son. And if I'd been a boy, they would have paid the fine!" she protested. She went on to deflect my rebuttal before I could even make it: "I know they think they need a boy to look after them when they're old, blah blah blah, but why didn't they realize that China would change? Why didn't they think that girls can look after them, too?"

I'd never heard her express anything but boredom at the topic of her antecedents; this sounded more like blame. "People make mistakes. Your birth mother should not have to pay for her whole life for making that mistake, which I don't think was a mistake at the time anyway," I opined.

And that really set Lucy off. "Why did they get pregnant in the first place? What happened to women's rights? Actually, I feel a little bit angry with them," she admitted.

At that point, Grace waded in to lighten the mood on a topic that she, for one, had zero interest in allowing to spoil her contemplation of a sizzling pot sticker. "I'd just ask them for thirteen years' worth of *hongbao* and be done with it," she quipped, referring to the red lucky-money envelopes that Chinese children get once a year at new year. "And anyway, you know I am a high-maintenance person, and I would probably think they were very poor," she said. Our life was in so many ways so normal, but our dinner table conversation was certainly anything but mundane.

"Mommy, please don't eat the brown one!" Grace was pleading for the reprieve of my lunch: a hunk of stir-fried dog haunch that I was determined to stomach, whatever the consequences to her psyche or to my digestion.

Culinary tourism was always part of my cultural education project for Grace and Lucy. I'd pursued it that day to far-flung Guizhou province in southern China: older, friendlier, prouder, and purer than denatured Shanghai. And home to some of the mainland's most determined dog eaters. That's how we ended up at Xiao Hong's dog diner in the Guizhou town of Panjiang—a town that, at the time, had nothing noncanine on its menu. And in the rigid hierarchy of Guizhou canine cuisine, brown was ranked tastiest, swiftly followed by black, Dalmatian, and white dog. So brown dog hot pot it would be, despite the fact that we had recently adopted Dumpling, a small brown mutt who had himself been rescued from a cooking pot in Shanghai.

I'm not sure why I thought inviting my girls to eat something that looked like our own beloved puppy back home would foster love of their homeland. I faintly recall thinking it was a good idea to expose them to as much cultural authenticity as possible while they were still young enough to tolerate it. I think I can safely say the passage of time has convinced me that I was wrong. It didn't give them any warm fuzzy feelings about China. In an essay she wrote years later, Lucy called it "scarring."

Grace refused even to enter the diner. She hid in our tour guide's minivan, crouching on the dirty floor munching Oreos, drinking lukewarm Sprite, and making sure she didn't accidentally spot any dog sinew out the window. Lucy came with me, and the first thing we both saw was a wok filled with a teeming mass of brown stuff, which we quickly realized were puppy paws in soy sauce. Lucy's only goal seemed to be to prove she was more courageous than her sister, so nothing could gross her out—including watching me choose my cut of canine thigh meat from the slab of slaughtered dog at the entrance to the diner. It looked a lot like leg of lamb.

Like termites and caterpillars, mopane worms and goat guts (and all the other proteins I've eaten in my life just to prove what a good trooper I am), one dog hot pot will probably be enough for a lifetime. The taste just wasn't good enough to overcome the feeling I was eating Lassie. And the girls won't forget it as long as they live, though they seem to blame it more on me than on China.

Puppy paws apart, I felt that my campaign to teach them to love China through their taste buds was going pretty well. I thought it was time to teach them to love China through its people, too. And the population shows to its best advantage not in crowded, frazzled Shanghai, but in the quiet rural countryside, I thought. So we set off to search for the "real" China—and its people—in Guizhou province.

I'd warned them in advance that this wouldn't be our usual China trip (i.e., a tour of famous temples and sacred mountains by way of low-rent video game parlors and seedy amusement parks). This time, we were going to see how Chinese peasants—maybe even their own birth parents—really lived. Tiger mom couldn't have said it better.

Pretty soon we were all standing knee deep in a paddy field and squishing water buffalo poop through our toes. In forty years of traveling the world, I've seldom had the sense of traveling so far back in history. We were staying in the small town of Kaili, whose name appropriately means "Let's go to the rice paddy field with the water buffalo." That's how we ended up helping the local Miao—one of China's fifty-five ethnic minority groups—plant their rice crop.

Unlike the Shanghainese (or, for that matter, New Yorkers), they hadn't lost their native sense of hospitality yet. So when we came upon our first field of Miao women planting rice seedlings, some of them in traditional headdress, they politely encouraged us to muck right in. Grace would later say one of her very few vivid memories of China was their elaborate indigo-blue headdresses worn over ragged farm clothes.

They were none too impressed by how squeamish Grace and Lucy were. Had my kids been blond and sunburned, the seven planting matrons would probably have given them more of a break. But because they looked exactly like Chinese peasant children, right down to the sunburned cheeks, the Miao moms seemed to think they ought to act like them, too.

"Don't waste," scolded the matriarch of the paddy field when one of my children dropped a precious seedling without planting it, not knowing it would yield half a pound of rice at harvest. All of us proved incompetent at planting seedlings upright in the mud at just the right intervals under more than an inch of water.

"I didn't realize something that simple could be fun," Lucy recalled years afterward. "This was how they were making a living, but it was really fun. They were like 'Don't drop it; this little seed could feed a whole family,' or whatever. It was gross and dirty, but they were so friendly!" she remembered. We had jeopardized their harvest, but they still spent half an hour trying to persuade us to stay for lunch.

We quickly realized that in Guizhou, hospitality was the default. "Come and drink tea," every villager would shout out as we passed an open doorway; every farmer went out of his or her way to step aside to let us pass as we traversed the dikes between the submerged rice fields. They were probably afraid we'd fall in if they didn't.

Of course, it was easy to confuse poverty with charm in a place like Guizhou. Its people were among the poorest in China. They farmed on seemingly vertical hillsides, terraced their fields nearly to the top of every available mountain, and ploughed by hand or with a draft animal—all backbreaking work. They carried crushing loads by shoulder pole, beat laundry with a stick in oft-polluted waterways, and every grandma seemed to have a sturdy toddler strapped to her back—offspring of the children she had lost to labor as migrant workers in a distant city. And they ate dog, not just because they liked it, but because starvation was not something distant and medieval, but a part of their living memory.

We called in at a local pottery, for example, just to show the kids how peasants used charred rice bran and quicklime from the nearby hills to make the dishes they ate from. But the elderly potter, the sixth generation of his trade, launched off instead into a narrative about the Great Leap Forward, Mao

Zedong's brilliant idea for boosting Chinese agricultural production, which contributed to a famine that killed millions of Chinese in the late 1950s and early 1960s. He spoke matter-of-factly about how his mother would go into the mountains each day, hoping to come back with roots and wild greens to feed her family and how that still wasn't enough to keep some of his younger siblings from starving to death.

The sixty-something famine survivor, a cheap local cigarette dangling from his lips, had his head bowed over a squeaky potter's wheel as he noisily slapped wet clay on the side of the next rice bowl, so between that and the fact that he spoke Mandarin with a very strong local accent, I didn't get all the details. But the message was clear: he still remembered the feeling of a belly filled with whatever was at hand. (Some Chinese peasants ate soil to fill their stomachs, dying when it blocked their intestines.) That's not the kind of history lesson my girls would have gotten in their international school in Shanghai. The trip was worth it, just for that.

"Want a live chicken with that?" It was 25 degrees below zero Fahrenheit on China's northern border with Russia, and the zookeeper's heart wouldn't melt any icicles, either. He was urging us to pluck a scrawny live bird out of the cage by his side. The idea was for Grace or Lucy to dangle the bird out our tour bus window so they could get up close and personal with a bunch of Siberian tigers while they dismembered it. Given my passion for delivering experiences of maximum cultural authenticity to my children, I was keen to show them how mainlanders entertained themselves in a wild animal park: by getting sprayed with chicken blood and sinew, it seemed. The kids called it gross, but I called it acculturation.

But we didn't have to go as far as the dog diner in Guizhou for lessons in animal abuse, with Chinese characteristics. Around the corner from our home, at the Shanghai Zoo, staff stood by as tourists fed chip packaging, the plastic from gelatin cups, and other indigestibles to the monkeys. And I could hardly claim to be innocent of it myself. I did, after all, name our dog Dumpling and think it was funny.

So when I heard that China had built a hotel with white tigers smack in the middle of the lobby, it seemed like a natural for us. There were tigers at check-in, tigers in the breakfast room, and an entire safari park next door where the kids could cuddle a baby tiger while feeding it infant formula from a bottle.

This was a weekend break with distinctly Chinese characteristics. An entire family of snow tigers—the kind without stripes—lived right next to the check-in desk. I was reliably assured by the staff that, though the hotel management would stop at nothing for my enjoyment, the tigers had not been bleached. It seems they were born that way. And in the breakfast room, a majestic trio of live white tigers were packed into a too-small glassed-in courtyard. They never stopped pacing. I didn't need my daughters to tell me that wasn't a good sign in a captive animal.

At the safari park, many of the tourists seemed more interested in staring at our multiracial family than at the giraffes. On the trolley through the nonpredator section, I was trying to figure out what the anteaters were up to, but the Chinese granny behind me was craning her neck at me instead, speculating at the top of her lungs about the provenance of the Asian-looking kid on my lap. She clearly viewed a white lady cuddling a Chinese kid as about as weird as a warthog with a hyena baby. I was under the impression we were both homo sapiens, but Granny didn't seem to think so.

We'd all need to carry our belongings on our backs, pee before we left home, and take along whatever sustenance we might need for the whole day. This was our first train trip during the peak Chinese New Year travel period. And I'd heard horror stories about it.

Fearing a massive crush of unruly migrants bearing goats, pigs, and new rice cookers back to their hometowns for new year, we left at 6:00 a.m. to get to the station an hour early. There, we found orderly queues of people, all rolling luggage (no one had backpacks but us), moving in a sedate fashion through security screening and the ticket barrier and onto the train without pushing, shoving, cutting in line, or stealing my handbag.

I'd had a complicated security plan. Children were to carry backpacks on their fronts to avert theft; one person was to be stationed at the back of the luggage X-ray machine and one at the front, to make sure no one walked off with my handbag or iPad after it was scanned. However, the cops prevented more than a sensible number of people from going through security at one time, so we didn't have to implement operation Waldmeirs-on-vacation. The only sign that the system was under any strain at all was when the station McDonald's ran out of Big Breakfasts. And when an overexcited toddler threw up in the row in front of us on the train, an immaculately coiffed train attendant cleaned it up in record time. It didn't even put the kids off consuming twenty-four hours' worth of snacks in four hours.

As usual I had chosen our holiday destination by just how Chinese it was. That meant I often chose a down-at-the-heels local resort—the more kitsch the better—because I figured that was where real Chinese people went to play. Exactly the kind of resort that would never exist once my kids were old enough to go there voluntarily.

From the station, we took an illegal taxi (there was no other kind), which drove on the wrong side of the road around blind bends in the rain, ignoring my bleating in my best Chinese the local equivalent of "Slow the heck down." We arrived at the seedy resort hotel I had chosen, again, for maximum authenticity, to find that we appeared to be the only guests. There was a stretch Hummer outside, though.

From then on, we flagged down any passing vehicle when we needed a lift, especially the loaf-of-bread-shaped minivans known as *mianbaoche*, which acted as unofficial taxis to the masses, and headed off to visit a local UNESCO heritage site where we could hike along a metal walkway dangling by a few rusty cables from the side of a sheer cliff. Back safely in our down-at-the-heels hotel, we curled up three to the fluffy king-size bed and watched *Beverly Hills Chihuahua* and *Dora the Explorer* in Chinese.

The discovery of a pack of condoms in the hotel bathroom led to a lively conversation about sex:

Mom:	"You two know what condoms are for, right?"
Grace:	"They are only ninety-seven percent effective, you know."
Mom:	"How did you know that?"
Grace:	"That's how Rachel got pregnant on *Friends*."

This was followed by a vigorous debate about how to translate the word *asshole* into Chinese, leading me to reflect, as I often did, on how important it was to visit depressing one-horse towns like the one we were in, Yandangshan, and stay in empty cavernous cold hotels with muddy shoeprints on the side of the bath and moldy shower curtains, just for the bonding.

Once the girls were preteens, it seemed that we did our best communicating when stuck somewhere with only Chinese television and preferably no Internet connection. It was certainly better than passing one another like ships in the Chinese night as we did on most weekdays, when the kids, if asked what they did at school, gave the international Esperanto signal for "nothing." Thank God for the lesser tourist attractions of China; they were perfect for family slumber parties.

Since it was cold and wet and miserable outside—and there was nowhere to go anyway—we chatted for hours that night, even broaching for the first time ever the topic of boys. Grace revealed that she wanted to die when she was ninety-seven—a life, according to her, that would be "not too long, because if you lived to a hundred and fourteen, you really might not want to go on any longer" but not too short, either. And Lucy made known that, if absolutely forced to have plastic surgery, she would get her little toe fixed because it "doesn't get acknowledged enough because no one can see it."

The next day, Chinese New Year's Eve, began with the kind of tepid buffet that seems to be de rigueur in Chinese hotels of a certain type. I consider it one of the seven wonders of the world that China, with one of the greatest cuisines on earth, can't do a breakfast buffet. This one was typical: chafing dishes without any fuel under them, lukewarm soup dumplings filled with partially congealed pig fat, topped off with stone-cold spring rolls and Kool-Aid masquerading as orange juice. Even the tea water was not really hot. The only thing marginally appealing was the dessert cart; let them eat cake, even if it's for breakfast.

We set off in another illegal taxi with a cheerful young driver who shared the flaw we often encountered when traveling in rural China: he could not keep his eyes on the road for staring at us. He wanted to know if my husband was Chinese and, when told the girls were adopted, wanted to know if we knew who their biological parents were. That provoked a conversation with the kids about birth parents, a topic we seldom broached except when traveling. Maybe it was all the staring.

On that occasion, Grace wondered aloud whether her birth grandmother on her mother's side had died of cancer from cigarette smoking since my mom did. Her logic was that so many people smoked in China, it was far from impossible.

On our way back from a visit to the area's stunning six-hundred-foot waterfall, we stopped at a glassblower's stall only to find that he, like many of the migrant workers we met in eastern China, was from Grace's hometown of Yangzhou. He presented the girls with free blown-glass mobile phone ornaments declaring, "They are my countrymen," and pointing out that even Lucy's hometown was only fifty miles from Yangzhou. One guy like that made up for all the staring.

"Just give her whatever price she asks for. She's North Vietnamese; we probably napalmed her grandmother when I was little." We were in the market for a pair of flip-flops to replace Grace's only set of footwear, which had just fallen to bits on our first trip to North Vietnam. But my heart just wasn't in the haggling. I was having cultural guilt pangs.

We had booked on China's first-ever luxury cruise to Vietnam, where all of us—me, my girls, and our Chinese cruise mates—pretty much counted as former imperialists.

My Chinese kids and I would have found ourselves on opposite sides in the Vietnam War, of course, and that war was a powerful influence on me when I was their age. I grew up counting body bags coming home from Vietnam and praying that my elder brother would pick a low enough draft number to avoid shipping off to kill Commies. (He did.) Then forty years later, I found myself drinking mocktails with a boatload of those very same Commies on a cruise ship off the coast of the country we once jointly conspired nearly to obliterate. It amused me no end to think that the Red Army officer I was chatting with would have had to shoot me if we'd run into each other back then. And I marveled again at the happy accident of politics and history that meant that after Beijing stopped demonizing us, they started giving us babies instead.

I'd tried to use the whole cruise thing as a teachable moment for my then-thirteen- and fourteen-year-old daughters, whose grasp of American history and geography was so tenuous that one had recently asked whether Florida was in California. Over Egg McMuffins at the airport on our way to board the ship, I'd dispensed a potted history of the Vietnam War, confident that something that had so torn apart my childhood could not help but fascinate my adoring daughters. Wrong again. "We don't care, Mom"—the classic comeback of the American teen, proof beyond all doubt that they really did only look Asian.

I had to remind myself that this whole "move to China" lark was as much about unconscious immersion in the culture of their birth as it was about teaching them anything specific, including language. Our relaxing sea cruise began, for example, with a boombox blasting on the gangplank because as any mainlander will tell you, the only genuine way to have fun in China is when things are *renao*, a word that can be loosely (and generously) translated as "loud and chaotic."

I was dismayed to find that the safety drill turned out to be an occasion for yet more *renao*. I'd dragged the kids down to the muster station expecting that they'd be shown how to don life vests and abandon ship, but we could barely hear above the din of passengers shouting into their cellphones. America and China, two nations separated by an ocean and united in spawning tourists that the rest of the world loves to hate.

Too soon, the cruise was ending—fittingly in Danang, which will always and forever be, for me, the place where the body bags came from. After four days in Vietnam, most of our fellow cruisers hadn't tasted a bite of Vietnamese food ("We don't dare!" one of them told me), or spent a cent of Vietnamese money. (They all used the mighty renminbi.) And most tellingly of all, in the streets of North Vietnam where we stopped to stroll, the beggars didn't even bother to try to shake me down. They only begged from the Chinese.

See, kids, didn't I tell you? One day you'll be glad I dragged you off to live in the world's next superpower. Those Vietnamese know an ugly American when they see one—except these days, the ones they see are all Chinese.

But for all our trips in search of the real China, perhaps the most Chinese trip of all did not involve the mainland or mainlanders at all. One spring break, Grace requested that we go to Taiwan: a place that is at once both where China was decades ago and where it could be again one day, if it's lucky. It's a modern, efficient, polite, friendly society, which has also managed to preserve the best of ancient China in its culture, traditions, and even (yum) foods. I've never met anyone who loved China who didn't love Taiwan even more, including a lot of mainlanders.

Not only do Taiwanese frown on any form of phlegm on public transport, but they take the whole civilization thing one huge step further: they reserve seats for the elderly, disabled, pregnant, or any other form of infirm citizen, but crucially, unlike those on the mainland, they also resist sitting in the reserved seats, even when sorely tempted at rush hour.

When our public bus pulled over to the side of the road along with all the other rush hour traffic to let an ambulance pass, we were amazed. The ambulance didn't even need to use a siren. Lights were enough, and afterward, drivers allowed one another to rejoin the flow of traffic without a drop of blood being spilled in the race to chase the ambulance. I turned to the kids and said, "In twenty years, Shanghai will be like this."

Grace replied, "And by then this place will be even better."

I really began to wonder whether bringing my Chinese kids to live in China had done anything but turn them into mainland haters. They could have learned to despise their homeland quite effectively just by staying home.

Taiwan even got us talking about Chineseness. On a hike in the island's stunning Taroko Gorge, which cuts through the aboriginal mountains of central Taiwan, we happened on the topic of whose army they would join if they were ever forced to take sides: The United States or China? Given their virulent Americanism, I thought it would be hands down for Uncle Sam, but both girls said it was a very tough choice. As we sweated up the narrow path between the limestone cliff and the rushing river far below, they even took the time to explain it to me. "If I fought for the United States, I might be killing one of my relatives," Lucy said. It was the first time I ever remember them showing anything like allegiance to China or even any sense of Chineseness.

We'd looked for it all over the mainland, from rundown resorts to rundown cruise ships, from rice paddies to dog diners. It seems we had to leave the country to discover the China in us.

I thought the best way to cement that sentiment, as always, would be to feed it. So we set off for the culinary heart of Taipei, the Shilin Night Market, where even finicky Grace could be won over by the Taiwanese habit of serving everything-on-a-stick, barbecued. The girls rented plastic fishing poles and bait, nabbing crayfish that they skewered and grilled themselves and fed to their adoring mother. Grace loved the meat sticks, *shengjianbao* with Taiwanese greens, and corn on the cob with five-spice powder. I swooned for the traditional Taiwanese slimy oyster omelets. We all loved the spiral-sliced whole potatoes, skewered on a stick and deep fried to make one giant potato chip. And who could resist Taipei Night Market's signature dish, penis-shaped waffles? We ended the evening with me getting a meat cleaver massage, a form of Chinese traditional medicine that involves being beaten on the back, shoulders, and even head by the blunt edge of a nine-inch cleaver. But all either of the kids ever remembered from that trip was the penis waffles.

CHAPTER 8

No Place Like Home

THE YANGZHOU GIRLS WERE NODDING off, tumbled together three to a double seat on the too-tall tour bus carrying them back to the city that did not want them.

"We are now crossing the Yangtze River," the tour guide intoned as the cobalt neon lights bordering Yangzhou's futuristic new highway reflected off the surface of the river, one of the oldest landmarks in China. It wasn't the kind of information to get schoolgirls squealing.

But soon one Yangster leaped from her seat with a shriek of, "Oooh, the Yangtze River!"

Another dug herself out of a jumble of her Yangzhou sisters' limbs to proclaim, "Yeah, that's, like, the place where we were born."

A dozen or more other Yangzhou girls, aged from eight to eighteen, let out what sounded like a communal sigh of satisfaction. They were about to visit the scene of the greatest tragedy of their young lives—the loss of mother and family and homeland at an age when other babies had not even been to the mall yet. And they seemed to be thoroughly looking forward to it.

With good reason: by the time Yang Shu Min (my daughter Grace) joined her two closest Yangzhou sisters, Yang Yuyao (Lily Mueller) and Yang Yilin (Natalie Petro) to go "home" to Yangzhou in 2009, Beijing was ready to make amends to babies like them for what will always be a blot on the image of China. The three Yangsters were nine years old—and what a difference nine years had made.

By then Beijing was eagerly throwing money—and toys, toys, toys—at all those banished babies to expiate the national guilt. It was offering free homeland trips, complete with over-the-top orphanage reunions, to tens of thousands of the lost daughters of China. Our 2009 trip was one such, put together to celebrate the twentieth anniversary of the Yangzhou orphanage. Some thirty-five other families came from the United States, the United Kingdom, Canada, the Netherlands, Denmark, and Sweden. My seventy-eight-year-old father flew in from Detroit, as did the family of Yang Yilin (including all four children, adopted and biological) and the mother and sister of Yang Yuyao. Think Hallmark, with Chinese characteristics.

In fact, Hallmark would probably have been more restrained. Every time our cavernous bus lumbered to a stop in Yangzhou, banners were unfurled for us, strewn with hearts and dripping with sentiments proclaiming eternal kinship with the misplaced daughters of Yangzhou. "Welcome Home!" they shrieked. "One Love, One Family" was the favored slogan. I couldn't help but imagine Communist Party cadres meeting in closed-door session for months to hammer out a new official attitude toward foundlings, complete with approved slogans. The new China would no longer bundle them away to orphan homes that most residents did not even know existed; they would be morphed into celebrities by official diktat.

"We are your family forever," the city's deputy mayor proclaimed, choking on the words, while we adoptive families looked askance at platters of artfully arrayed duck heads. In a country where government officials normally seem chosen by their ability to say nothing at great length, it was already a major departure from precedent for a mandarin to speak from the heart like this. "Thirty-six Yangzhou babies, though living far from their hometown, have traces of China inside them," he went on to declaim, in between alternating choruses of "There's No Place Like Home" and "Auld Lang Syne" performed by a lady in a pink frock crooning from behind a curtain of bubbles. But just when I was worried that he might take the whole ethnic reclamation project too far, he veered off to announce the puppet and magic shows. Just a passing mention of the fact that once a Chinese, always a Chinese. How could I, of all people—I who had moved my whole family to the motherland to honor that same basic principle—begrudge him pointing that out?

Luckily for the kids, they discovered that Yangzhou was not just renowned for culinary delicacies that their picky palates couldn't stomach—the recipe for one famous Yangzhou dish begins with the words "Start with oil from the ovaries of ten old chickens"—but also for its stuffed animals. So when their hometown wasn't honoring them with foods they'd never eat in a million years, it was burying them under piles of life-size teddy bears and brocade-covered bulls chosen to celebrate that year's zodiac animal. Floppy stuffed animal limbs protruded from parental luggage overstuffed with mementos, from China-red pashminas to Great Wall paperweights, all of it designed to let no one forget that China loved its children, even the ones it exported to other countries.

Grace, Lily and Natalie return together to visit their orphanage

What did the Yangsters think about all that? Their hometown had them at the teddies. Discarded less than a decade ago, they were coming back as rock stars. Luckily, most of them were far too young to grasp the irony.

Three infants in three mugshots, all clad in what seemed to be a regulation foundling pullover with one wide stripe across the chest, the uniform of babies living in a world where food, diapers, and naps only arrived when the timetable said so.

Grace, Lily and Natalie were clutching these three thumbnails, their official adoption photos, and giggling hysterically. Lily's mouth was open wide and her eyes squeezed shut in a shriek of utter delight. Grace's eyes were doing that thing she hates when she smiles in photos: disappearing into slits. Natalie grinned and ducked to avoid the spray from the new orphanage fountain that was generating a curtain of mist in the background. For once, Grace wasn't moaning about being asked to pose for pictures.

A few feet away was what the orphanage called its Love Wall: a giant collage of the official adoption photos of all the kids ever adopted from Yangzhou. Each child present that day had autographed her photo. Grace had signed both her English and Chinese names, and I was egotistically proud of her for doing so. Later, the Yangsters would make plaster casts of their handprints; the orphanage used them to build a wall to commemorate what happened there. Where other children have intimate family portraits shot in the hospital delivery room or iPhone screenshots of their mother's ultrasound scan, ours had a wall full of plaster of Paris handprints and a collage of standardized baby photos. And they could not have been less troubled by it.

Like the healthy, well-balanced nine-year-olds they were, they lived in the moment of their latest jest, game, or roughhousing opportunity. For them, our 2009 Yangzhou trip was first and foremost a reunion of three little girls who'd been friends since they were babies. If someone wanted to give them teddies and get all choked up about it, well, that was their business.

I did choke up like clockwork. I cried when we stepped off the coach to a platoon of female kettle drummers dressed in space-age pleather, and I gulped at the sight of battalions of nannies in pink uniforms with the telltale creases of packages that are only ever opened to impress guests. Watching our

Yangzhou girls crowd around a blue-skinned infant foundling with a hole in her heart, I had to turn away. And when the Yangsters posed next to the very cribs they had shared as infants, I crumpled.

I was not the only one. Grace commented, bemused, to fellow Yangster Natalie, "Many parents are crying, but we're just laughing," and then went on to chide me one more time for weeping. I did so much of it that she felt moved to explain to her Yangzhou friends that this was nothing to worry about, since Mom often cried "because she is so happy she got me."

Like every adoptive parent who takes her child back to any orphanage in China, I feared a reality overdose. But there were so many life-size cartoon figures roaming the orphanage grounds, so many saccharine sweets and even more saccharine speech making (including by me—I made a speech in Mandarin on behalf of the parents) that reality hardly got a look in. The day was hot, and the speeches were boring, and there were inevitable meltdowns among children who'd had too little sleep or too much stimulation, but almost none of the kids showed any negative reaction to the place itself or even to the calamity that put them there in the first place.

"It's cool!" That was the verdict of Lily Mueller, the Yangster who had been so thrilled at her first sighting of the Yangtze. "The nannies hold the babies like they are their own daughters."

Natalie Petro, a girl of few words, said the place was "really nice" and meant it.

They all seemed touched by the warmth of the homecoming, and said in an offhand way that they enjoyed seeing the nannies who looked after them. But clearly none of them remembered any of the staff—they were only eight months old when we got them—and equally clearly, the nannies didn't recall them, either. Idle curiosity was manifest on both sides, nothing more than that.

Still, the mothers of Natalie and Lily reported a bit of limited fallout later on. On a visit to the orphanage's communal squat toilet—a reality check if ever there was one—Lily gripped her mother's hand as she perched precariously above the evacuation hole and proclaimed with as much enthusiasm as she ever mustered for the Yangtze, "I'm glad you didn't leave me here!"

Natalie, when asked if she would have minded spending her life there, said, "It might have been fun growing up around so many other children," but she was still extremely eager to get "home" to America.

I scrutinized their behavior, interrogated them about their feelings, and tried to read the tea leaves of their sleeping and eating patterns, looking for some profound reaction to this first real collision with their life story. I didn't find much. Maybe our girls were simply too young to articulate, or even to notice, how they felt about the place.

Beijing seemed worried that many of these kids could end up in therapy. One Chinese official who traveled with us to Yangzhou even suggested the reunions were partly intended as international group therapy sessions. "We want them to know that, though they had to be adopted, it wasn't because the people of their hometown didn't care about them," he told me as I took shelter from the unseasonably hot March sunshine. "We're afraid the children may suffer long-term psychological harm unless they can be persuaded that they were valued and cared for, both by the nannies at the orphanage and by the town itself," he said earnestly. Bit late for that, I thought. Surely the reunions were more public relations therapy than anything else, a chance to disprove the conventional global wisdom that all Chinese people hate girls. Maybe some cadres even saw it as a way to scoop up donation dollars from grateful parents. Still, I was happy for the Chinese government to shell out for a pair of rose-tinted spectacles through which my kids could view the dark facts of their lives. It was certainly better than the alternative.

After we left the orphanage that day, as Grace, Lucy, and I slumped exhausted in our rock-hard king-size bed in a local hotel, Grace fussed at the plight of a disabled eighteen-year-old who had never been adopted and was then a cook at the orphanage. She had taught Grace to make dumplings earlier that day. "Why is she still there?" Grace wanted to know.

"Back then, there were so many healthy infants that kids like her were left out," I explained, provoking Grace to ask whether the fact that she herself was a bed-wetter when little could have caused her to be classed as disabled. I told her that at eight months old, even Beijing couldn't expect her to be potty trained. Reassured, she had not the slightest interest in any further postmortem.

I asked how it would be if she'd never been adopted.

"Odd," was all she said. For in her world back then, in the presence of her Yangzhou sisters, nothing could be more normal than being the adopted Chinese daughter of a dumpy old white lady. It was everyone else who was odd. I might have had an emotional experience at the orphanage, but Grace had had a chance to miss school and hang out with her friends.

By then, the Yangzhou girls had been on so many vacations together, celebrating every birthday together from that first one and whooping it up every year on Gotcha Day, too, that they were closer to one another than to some cousins-by-adoption. Lily's mother, Tonia Mueller, and I had taken our troop of four Chinese toddlers to the zoo so often that we took out a joint membership—one intended for same-sex couples, but we probably spent as much time there together as if we were married. We'd braved Disney World together, losing Lily's four-year-old sister from China in the scrum and jointly panicking over it, and virtually every long weekend, Tonia and her husband Klaus generously hosted us at their vacation home near the Chesapeake Bay, where Papa Mueller taught Grace a lifelong love of fishing.

All this togetherness made for great photo albums. From that first portrait of infants slumped against the wall, we have year after year of Yangs, lined up on whatever couch we could find, usually in the same order as on that first day. We have them riding ponies on the Mueller family farm in Western Maryland, at the zoo and the pool and the beach and the amusement park and even on the New York subway. Even after we moved to China, the Muellers hosted a reunion of two or three of the Yangzhou girls and their Chinese sisters every time we came back to the United States.

It is no hyperbole to say I love them all like daughters, and whenever I faced a crisis with my own children, even in China, the Yangzhou parents were the first ones I'd call for advice. I feel bound to them with ties that are almost like kinship, right down to the feuding. My father and stepmother, elder brother and younger half siblings, aunt, uncles, and cousins could not have been more loving to my Chinese girls. But the Yang extended family had something that the Waldmeir extended family did not have: a child to raise who didn't look like them.

But how had we all ended up in such an improbably constituted extended family in the first place? That's what we all wanted to know when we gathered in Beijing at the start of that Yangzhou reunion trip. Why did China give me Grace and not Lily or Maya? Why Lucy and not Tonia's younger daughter, Maggie, both of them from Anhui province? How did they pick the perfect kids for me?

"Oh, that's simple," we were told outside the mysterious matching room in Beijing, where bureaucratic alchemists take one dusty manila file from one teetering stack, mix it with another from the neighboring stack, and presto, love is born. The lady bureaucrat took one look at me, Grace, and Lucy and said, "You all look alike. You have the same chin." Thank God for physiognomy.

And then on the final night of our stay in Yangzhou, the city sent its lost American daughters out to see how the other half of the Yangzhou family lived. Through the fairy-lit waterways and under the humpbacked bridges of their 2,500-year-old hometown, the Yangzhou Americans went out to meet the true Yangzhounese.

In the back lanes of the town, where electric scooters roared uncomfortably close to old grannies teetering on pedal bikes, where grandfathers groaned under shoulder poles loaded with purple sweet potatoes while chatting on their cellphones, life went on at the sweet slow pace that the Yangsters' hometown is known for. Each of the returning girls and her family were farmed out to a family of locals.

The Petro family of six—Mom, Dad, two older biological sons, and two adopted Chinese daughters—were picked up for dinner in a Hummer. The Muellers were invited to pick strawberries on their hosts' family farm, and when one member of the American branch of the family struggled with chopsticks, a member of the Yangzhou branch rushed off on a bicycle to buy a fork and spoon for her. The family with the Hummer felt no repast was complete without fireworks, so they sent out for some midmeal. And in the modest flat that the Yang-Waldmeirs visited, home of a Yangzhou television cameraman and his university professor wife, a daughter almost exactly the same age as Grace was being raised with almost exactly the same range of noisy electronic toys.

As the hostess and I chatted in her galley kitchen before the meal—which included Grace's Chinese favorite, *hongshaorou* (red cooked pork belly), made in the special Yangzhou style—it became clear that Yangzhou had been growing up right along with our girls. These were the heady days right after the 2008 Beijing Olympics. China was on top of its game, economically strong at a time when the rest of the world economy was still wobbling. And every Chinese parent in Yangzhou had the certainty that so many Western parents lacked back then: that their children's lives would be so much better than theirs had been.

All this prosperity had had its impact on the baby business, too; adoptions from Yangzhou had plummeted. The institution had so few healthy infants to place that it had begun adopting out nearly all its older children, including one ten-year-old who returned with us that day and many with special needs. Those who remained were toddlers with correctible or minor special needs, who likely would find homes, and severely disabled children, who would not. By the time of our visit, eighty-odd special-needs kids were living at Yangzhou in a brand new four-story building decked out more like a resort than an orphanage. Even more astoundingly, they were evenly divided between boys and girls.

By then, the shortage of healthy infant girls—the stuff of Chinese abandonment for centuries and fuel of international adoptions for decades—had led to a dramatic drop in overseas adoptions from China. And the gender ratio of adoptees has also changed dramatically, from 97 percent girls when we adopted the Yangsters to 63 percent in 2009.

So what did Grace take away from our Yangzhou home visit? "It made me wonder how my birth parents really live now," Grace said in bed afterward. "My birth mom might have been poor when she abandoned me, but since everyone in Yangzhou is so rich these days, maybe she's richer than us now!" I'd been afraid our visit might trigger a tsunami of complicated emotions in Grace, but what it provoked instead was just plain healthy greed. Maybe one day, she would grieve for what happened to her there, but at age nine, it was pretty clear that she didn't feel the need of a birth mother to be happy, just an iPhone.

It was back to school in Shanghai after that, back to a flat that felt increasingly like home, and back to our normal lives, which, Grace opined, seemed to differ very little from those of our Yangzhou host family, except that our beds were softer.

For one thing, like other Chinese kids (and unlike Americans their age), my girls were allowed to buy their very own set of fireworks each lunar new year and stay up till dawn blowing things up. "You don't seriously think I'd be letting you risk blowing your arm off if we were living back in America?" I pointed out one year when they were whining about being in China. Some children just never realize how lucky they are to live in a country without explosives litigation.

And then there was Christmas. One of the best things about living overseas was that we could cancel all of it, bar the presents. One year, we even canceled Christmas dinner; instead, each of us ordered what she most fancied. Grace had pizza, I had a Big Mac (delivered by twenty-four-hour McDonald's home delivery), and Lucy ordered chicken wings. And we all had dessert before we ate our main course. The kids got their presents (typically, electronics purchased ahead of time in the United States every summer on our home leave), but we only put up the sorriest excuse for an artificial tree and strung only colored lights on it; no fussy tinsel or fragile bulbs to hang. Our sole decoration was an illuminated eight-foot inflatable Christmas bear for our tiny front lawn. We stayed in our pajamas all day and left the next day for skiing in Korea. No dishes, no church, no arguments, nothing but a family spending the day together exactly the way they wanted to spend it. Who knew there could be so many unexpected benefits of Chineseness?

So we all tried to find the best of both worlds to celebrate about our lives in China. The low crime rate was a big plus; from the age of ten and eleven, Grace and Lucy were perfectly safe going to school alone by taxi. We even counted on the Chinese Communist Party to protect us from the terrorist attacks that multiplied in Europe and the United States while we lived overseas.

Grace still complained about disliking China, but when teachers, relatives, and friends asked why, she often struggled to explain cogently. "At home, we could just run down the street and play with our friends whenever we wanted to," she once told my father. This was hugely ironic since "at home" we had lived on a busy road that neither child was ever allowed to walk along, whereas in Shanghai, we lived in a Norman Rockwell painting of a place where cars had to navigate an intricate maze of flowerpots to make sure they never exceeded five miles per hour.

But in every other way, Grace was still living in America, virtually. (No) thanks to social media, she lived like an all-American girl, just accidentally growing up in China. As with American girls her age everywhere, that meant a lot of swooning over the boy band One Direction.

We chose the itinerary of almost every overseas trip based on where One Direction would be performing. And even if Grace couldn't make it to the concert, she insisted we spend a good chunk of our holiday time stalking the band or, in one case, even its merchandise bus. Kept informed by the tools of social media that she somehow managed to access in China, even when no one else could, she always knew where the best stalking was.

We spent one entire day chasing the One Direction merchandise bus through Australia's Gold Coast and another cruising the Las Vegas strip in a rented camper van looking for a sighting of the band, while Grace frantically tried to pretend she was not actually traveling in a motor home. One year, Lucy and I spent hours lurking in a cheap rental car outside the suburban Detroit hotel where the boys were rumored to be staying while Grace, thirteen, waited for a sighting and pretended she didn't know us. And then, finally, one of our former Shanghai neighbors sent Grace to boy-band heaven by arranging for her to attend a One Direction meet and greet near New York City. Grace took Yangzhou sister Lily along. But the real expert on this quintessentially Western phenomenon, the boy band, was not Yang Yuyao from the United States of America, but Yang Shu Min from China.

Grace even managed to plug into the worst parts of American culture. When she was twelve, her homeroom class at the bilingual international school she attended from ages eight to sixteen had a mini epidemic of cutting: teen girls deliberately carving up their skin to relieve psychic pain. Grace said she just wanted to try it once "to see what it felt like." Then she convened her own impromptu group therapy sessions, there in her middle school homeroom, to help the other kids get over the cutting epidemic. She displayed, as always, wisdom and empathy beyond her years. I've always wondered whether she was born with more understanding of human nature than the rest of us or whether adoption helped her to it.

Later, when a global Justin Bieber fan club called for mass suicides to protest his decision to smoke marijuana, Grace stayed up until midnight counseling girls halfway around the world on why they should not kill themselves. I guess teen angst knows no borders.

Then, she when was thirteen, just in time for a school trip to Italy, I bought my firstborn her first condoms. My logic was that it was never too soon to protect her against HIV and that a teen abortion could be more devastating to a child of abandonment than to the rest of us. I insisted she pack the prophylactics, only to hear later that that the boys on the trip (mostly ethnically Chinese) filled them with water and slung them at one another. That's another blessing of living in China; when you do something stupid like that, other parents just think it's because you're a foreigner. You don't automatically become a parenting pariah for giving thirteen-year-olds condoms to play with.

So Grace grew, but her interest in her backstory, for the most part, did not. The slightest minutiae of the lives of Niall, Harry, Louis, Liam, and Zayn (of One Direction) counted far more in her world than ethnicity, adoption, or certainly schoolwork. And as far as I could see, that was exactly as it should be.

About a month after we returned home from Yangzhou, when we were all lying in my king-size bed chatting on a Saturday night, Lucy, then eight, asked each of us what three things would we wish for if we could have anything on earth. For her part, she wanted "superpowers and magic, lots of pets, and no homework." I wanted to spend more time with the kids and to go horseback riding and hiking. And Grace? She ticked off being rich and famous and then paused before saying in a very small voice, "I'm sure this can never happen, but I'd like to see my birth mother." Those are the words that no adoptive mother, whatever her protestations to the contrary, ever wants to hear: she wants her, not me; I'm not good enough. Grace, blessed with a gift of intuition toward the feelings of others, immediately rushed to reassure me. "I just want to see what she looks like and let her know that I'm OK." I geared up for a major family therapy session on the topic of birth parent angst, but it was movie night, and Grace didn't want to waste any more time talking about some woman who "probably can only speak Chinese anyway." She ditched the subject to move on to the Coke and chips and cheap DVDs.

Still, for all that she lived in an America of the mind, every new kid at school immediately wanted to know why she looked Chinese and was called Waldmeir. "Mom, when you adopted us, did you have to pay money?" she asked me one school day when the alarm had just rung its 7:00 a.m. reveille. I froze packing up the lunches and stalled for time; could I really delve deep into explaining Chinese baby trafficking before I'd had my first Starbucks?

"Just a sec, honey, lemme get breakfast started, and then I'm happy to tell you all about it," I said, though I certainly wasn't. But I gamely dove into a forensic account of exactly how much I had indeed paid to procure her: $18,000, for travel, translation, and legal services, including a $3,000 "donation" to the orphanage. "When I adopted Lucy, her orphanage had no heating, though Anhui is very cold, and your orphanage had no air-conditioning, though Yangzhou is very hot, so the money went to pay for those things," I babbled. Even after years of fearing such a question, I had somehow not properly prepared for it. "Partly because of donations like that, your orphanage now has flat-screen televisions and underfloor heating." I summed up my case somewhat defensively.

So why was she asking anyway? "My friend at school has an adopted Chinese sister, and he says it cost a lot of money," Grace explained. I thought it was about time I told her that some orphanages (although not hers and Lucy's, I rushed to reassure her) used donations for less legitimate purposes—like lining the director's retirement account. "And there have been stories in the papers about some orphanage directors taking babies away from their birth families just so they can get skim off the donations that people like me are required to pay when they adopt."

"Oh, is that all?" Grace asked. "I thought maybe they raped them." And that was the last conversation we ever had about money and adoption.

Grace was scowling at me again. We were back in Yangzhou for another orphanage reunion. It was 2011, and Grace was eleven. The orphanage only had thirty resident kids by then, many severely disabled. The orphanage staff had taken us to visit, for the third time in our lives, Grace's finding place. The official forms said it was "Yangzhou East Lake bathroom," directly beside the local Wulimiao police station.

And that was why Grace was scowling. I was standing on the side of a dusty Chinese road, oblivious to the stares of everyone from rickshaw cyclists to Mercedes chauffeurs, and bawling at the sight of the place where she was left at six days old—and for the fact that no one remembered anything about that day. Grace and I had just been to the police station next door, where a brusque policewoman with a tight uniform and a loose perm told us that her police report was too old to be kept at the station any more, and it couldn't be located in the provincial storehouse. Half of me had been hoping the paperwork would help us trace the person who found Grace, since the finding person's name would surely be recorded there. But the other half was quite sure I didn't want to know. What if the finder knew the birth parents? Sometimes Pandora's box is better left unopened, especially in China.

Still, I wanted to know that someone had noticed my baby lying in the street that day. The policewoman volunteered that she herself had worked at the station back then, but no, she didn't remember anything about a baby abandoned there; and no, it wasn't exactly a daily occurrence even then to discover a foundling on the doorstep; and no, she really wasn't prepared to keep talking about this much longer. The only one more bored than she appeared to be Grace herself. "Oh, Mom, don't start crying again," she said, refusing for the umpteenth time to pose for another finding place photo. Been there, done that, she seemed to say.

At best, adoption was a haphazard affair back then. Yangzhou was receiving and adopting out more than a hundred abandoned baby girls every year. If it was anything like other orphanages in China, few if any records were kept of the babies until they were processed for adoption, usually several months later. No photographs were taken until one was needed to send to Beijing to match with a prospective parent. In many cases, no records were kept of the actual place, date, or time of abandonment. Many a police report was made up after the fact, once it was needed as part of the adoption paperwork (or, in some cases, faked for more nefarious reasons). Even in the aboveboard cases, no one cared what child was abandoned where and when. Adoption officials could never see why any of us adoptive parents cared about it.

And that was our last trip together to Yangzhou. I had been happy to take an eight-year-old there, and a nine-year-old, and even an eleven-year-old. But as Grace became a teenager, she had less and less interest in having a relationship with the city that could not keep her. I tried to give her the tools to bond with it by making sure she had fond memories of it, of her orphanage sisters, and of Yangzhou's *baozi* and chocolate fountains, which first began to soften her up to its charms. But I couldn't convert her, heart and mind, to her hometown. That, I figured, was her business.

CHAPTER 9

Baby Donuts

"WHERE WAS THE BABY LYING? How'd you find her? What was in the carrier bag? Did you see the mother? What's wrong with the baby? Where is she now?" The questions were tumbling from the lips of my elder child, the one who felt everyone's pain, the one who had always been fascinated by tragedy. Still awake well past her bedtime on a pre-Christmas night, eleven-year-old Grace was as transfixed as a preteen could possibly be by the unlikely tale I'd come home to tell, of the baby I found in the alleyway.

I'd crawled straight into bed with our dog Dumpling (himself abandoned on the streets of Shanghai as a puppy and named for the fact that he nearly became lunch for some peckish security guards), and I couldn't stop crying long enough to tell Grace clearly what had happened. Normally, she wouldn't stand for such waterworks, but that time she was tolerating me for the sake of the extraordinary story. She had even weaned herself away from her usual Saturday night multitasking: watching Australian Junior Master Chef via satellite television from the Philippines while group chatting to virtual friends from Orlando to Jakarta.

"Mr. John saw her while he was chaining his bike to the railings outside the Dunkin Donuts on Shimen Yi Lu, you know that one downtown that's close to the Marks and Spencer where we bought the Christmas crackers, down the street from the Awfully Chocolate where we got Lucy that really expensive birthday cake, remember?" She remembered the cake. Grace was a major connoisseur of cakes, and days would be spent before each birthday sampling the offerings of every Shanghai cake emporium before settling on the perfect one for that year.

Grace and Lucy had been to that Dunkin Donuts with me before, but by the ages of ten and eleven, they were old enough to stay home alone in our gated, guarded compound when I went off every Saturday night to a meditation meeting patronized mostly by foreigners: my dual fix of sugar and spirituality. That may be why the baby was abandoned there; doubtless, the desperate parents thought anyone foreign enough to like doughnuts and meditation was also rich and charitable enough to cure the child they could not care for.

"John came in and plonked down on the bench beside me and said, 'There's a baby outside,'" I told Grace and Lucy, dissolving in more sobs. I was already inside, licking sugar glaze off my cinnamon swirl roll, but I wiped my sticky fingers and followed him outside to the dank, dark alleyway that ran the length of the building, trailing away into the tangle of lanes and lean-tos that lay behind every skyscraper façade in Shanghai. "And there was a baby tied up with a rope, lying on top of some carrier bags," I told my rapt children.

"I couldn't tell at first if it was a boy or a girl." I didn't mention that I immediately knew why the baby was there, that yet again, a desperate mother had swaddled her newborn infant tight against the winter cold and left it alone in the night so that it could have a chance to live. Just another Grace or Lucy.

Their mothers did this, too, I thought instantly. Their mothers found a bit of cloth and bundled their hours-old bodies deep into it before knotting a rope around it to keep the predators away. Their mothers nursed them, maybe for the first and only time, before boarding a bus or a cart or maybe even a bicycle to take them to the place where babies who need new mothers go. Their mothers did this, too. How could they?

What were the odds, I thought, that I of all people would be forced to bear sad witness to this most mundane of Chinese tragedies? Couldn't someone else be there for it? Someone who didn't feel personal pathos right down to the bone every time this baby whimpered? Someone who didn't see Grace's tiny worried brow on its face and Lucy's perfect fingernails on its newborn hands? Someone who didn't feel ill at the very thought of how this child's fate had just been transformed, profoundly and forever?

By the time I got there, she was choking herself with indignation, but everyone nearby was pretending not to notice. Bystanders knew that to get involved would just bring problems. They could be accused of baby trafficking. Things were different for me as a foreigner; no one was going to accuse me of anything if I cuddled her. So I scooped her up and hung on tight. I couldn't breathe for weeping.

And thus Baby Donuts was born: a child whose abandonment would mark me as profoundly as that of my very own children.

Every detail of the scene spoke of maternal care and anguish: the multicolored quilt, bright, new, a corner laid over the child's face to protect her from the weather; the two plastic carrier bags beneath the angry bundle, bulging with pastel baby clothes, cans heavy with infant formula, crinkly packages of diapers, and cheap baby bottles smelling of new plastic. I clung on even tighter and sobbed.

I wept for Baby Donuts's mother, but I cried even harder for the birth mothers of Grace and Lucy, who may never know their daughters are safe and cherished beyond all measure. And I sobbed at the thought of all those bystanders who doubtless stood by pretending that Grace and Lucy weren't squalling back then, too.

I had cried for their birth mothers before, on my children's birthdays each year, when I always wondered if their first mothers were wondering about the babies they once bore. But I had never grieved as I did holding little Baby Donuts and for days afterward whenever I thought of her.

Did Grace and Lucy get the awful parallels with their own life stories? I wondered. But by then I'd declared a moratorium on guessing what they were thinking until they were old enough to tell me themselves. So I stuck to what was obvious. I could tell that they felt a sort of psychic bond with their sister in abandonment, but it was also pretty clear that they had no idea why it had so upset me. To them, abandonment was just a fact of life—of their lives. I was the one who had taught them to think that way, so I couldn't complain if they failed to see that every happy adoptive family is born of tragedy.

"Why didn't you bring her home?" Grace asked, perplexed. The last thing she wanted was a baby sister, but she couldn't stand the thought of that baby in that alleyway. Of course, I did consider stealing her. A tiny infant, struggling to breathe, screaming for her life? Who wouldn't want to grab her and run, through Saturday night streets flooded with neon and partygoers, to the doctor, to the hospital, to the help her birth parents either could not or would not pay for.

But I knew I couldn't just walk off with this unintended consequence of the one-child policy. I had friends who'd tried that. They'd rushed an abandoned baby onto a plane for an operation without which she would surely have died and then fought for years to get the paperwork to adopt her. I knew I had to let the system do its job: get her the crucial police report for her "certificate of abandonment," without which she could never be adopted. I knew the best gift I could give Donuts would be to make sure her paperwork was flawless.

But paperwork was one thing, and finding a squirming, squalling baby on one of the richest streets in the richest city in China was quite another. It unnerved me. I cuddled her, wondered idly if she needed a diaper change, and thought vaguely about giving her a bottle. But mostly, I just clutched her too hard. And then, suddenly, a gangly young ambulance worker was there to pick her up. He jostled her before settling her awkwardly in his arms—it was obviously the first time he'd held a baby that young—and she didn't like that. I wondered resentfully why they hadn't sent someone competent to pick up my baby.

The list of things I didn't do that night was long: I didn't take photos of the carrier bags filled with little love tokens. I didn't even do a thorough search for the note that might have been at the bottom of the bag and might later have been her most cherished possession. I knew such notes were sometimes written by birth parents on a scrap of red paper, recording just the date and time of birth or maybe pleading for help from strangers. I also knew notes like that often went missing or were discarded or ignored by orphanage officials who, for some reason, just don't get why the child might someday want it. I really should have looked for it.

So I missed a few tricks that night, and she may one day blame me for that. But I also vowed that, though I was too old, too single, and had too many children already to be Donuts's mother, I would be the next best thing: a self-appointed guardian who would advocate for her medical care, pay for it if necessary, and love her from the bottom of my heart until she had someone else to do it.

And I promised, too, that I would one day tell Baby Donuts her story—the story my own children may never know. I would make sure she knew that her mother chose a mild night after a run of freezing evenings, that she picked a busy time at the doughnut shop, and most of all, the one thing that I can never tell my own children with certainty, that her mother loved her. Because if it was not love lurking among the diapers and bottles and baby clothes, I have never seen love before. I hoped one day that she would think about those things and forgive the mother who left her there.

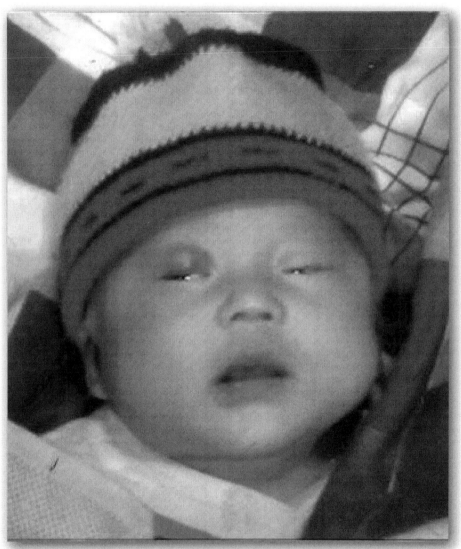

The baby in the alleyway, on the night she was discovered

I knew I'd lose all link to her if I didn't move fast. My friend John Fearon, the official finding person, had gone to the police station that night to give evidence, and he texted the only photo we had of her, along with the police report and the information that she likely had a heart defect. Within hours friends and family around the world had seen this digital thumbnail of a baby with a lump on one eye, a crocheted cap with golden pompom on top, and a mouth puckered with the struggle to let enough air in. And they pledged to make her whole again.

But first I had to find her. And for that, I roped in Grace and Lucy as accomplices. It seemed like a good idea at the time. Clutching the hands of my two Chinese daughters as some unspoken proof of goodwill, I made the rounds of the local pediatric wards, brandishing that sole blurry mobile phone photo for identification. The clothing was unique—a red, black and gold beanie, purple and brown patchwork bunting and pink quilted baby jacket— but the clothes would be long gone, I realized, swapped for anonymous pediatric nightgowns. Still, there was a big purple lump on her right eyelid, surely that would help me find a baby with no name, no birth date, no identity number, and no parents in a hospital system serving twenty-three million people.

So on the coldest night of the year, Grace, Lucy, and I trudged down to the corner convenience store and paid way too much for a dusty gift box of Lindt truffles from the highest shelf behind the cashier, aiming to use them to soften up the nurses. "Ah, Mom, why do I have to go? You know I hate hospitals." Grace desperately wanted to meet the baby she had heard so much about, but her mind's eye was freaking out at the imagined sight of severed limbs lying on hospital floors and the whole panoply of horrors she believed were to be found inside even the most advanced Chinese medical center.

Grace would not even watch the movie *Avatar* with us because she thought it was too scary. She had refused to visit me when I'd been hospitalized briefly the year before and had been telling me since she could talk that she did not plan to attend my funeral; illness and death had always terrified her. Lucy, for her part, was just bored by the whole outing.

So I promised them a treat on the way home, and we hopped a taxi, braving the inevitable taxi driver primer on the rights and duties conferred by adoption on the way to Shanghai's oldest children's hospital where I had intel that Donuts was being treated. I figured I would just use Grace and Lucy to get in the front door and then stash them in a coffee—or a doughnut—shop until I had checked up on Donuts's condition. But we were rebuffed from the start. At the front desk, the battle-ax in charge denied that the hospital even had a pediatric inpatient unit which, it being a children's hospital and all, seemed unlikely.

Then we found ourselves in pediatric emergency. That didn't go down well with Grace. Chinese hospitals don't confine illness to consulting rooms; it spills out into floors and corridors. But I plunged on anyway, dragging the kids up dingy staircases and down hallways filled with wailing, diverting to another corridor if there were any sick kids on public view. I told my sad story to every nurse and orderly, but they were far too busy to help me find that particular needle in a Chinese haystack. Eventually, we went home and ate the chocolates.

This clearly wasn't the world that my kids were born into; it was a new, less mendicant China. I was told in no uncertain terms that if one of China's babies needed help, China would be there to assist her. The middle kingdom didn't need people like me anymore—and neither did Donuts.

But maybe I needed her. I wanted to see for myself that she was safe, sound, and breathing without puckering her lips in that way that babies do when their hearts can't deliver enough oxygen. My kindhearted Chinese colleague Shirley Chen was on the case, too. While the girls and I escaped to Hong Kong for the holidays, she stayed home, gently rattling the cages of everyone she could think of who might bring her news of Baby Donuts. She was told that it was none of her business.

I began to despair that I would ever know if Donuts lived or died—and all because China had suddenly learned to resent the hand that donated to it. Beijing was willing to tolerate those of us who helped out when there was no alternative. But by then, offering help was viewed as offensive.

And the problem went deeper than that. Shanghai officials simply couldn't understand why I wanted to see her again, anyway. They assumed babies like her would never even be told they were adopted, let alone want to know anything about the circumstances. I knew differently, of course. I couldn't pretend my kids weren't adopted, even if I wanted to. How otherwise would I explain why they look so Chinese? And whatever her eventual parents told Donuts about her antecedents, I knew the parents themselves would want every shred of information about her beginnings because I knew I would kill to have that information about my own daughters. I still felt responsible for her.

I played my last card. I told the Shanghai government that I planned to write an article about Donuts, in which I might find it necessary to mention that I couldn't find her. Government officials quickly located the baby and reported on her condition; she had atrial septal defect (a hole in her heart), and a large angioma on her right eye. After becoming an instant expert on the conditions via WebMD, I didn't think they seemed life threatening. I was in the United States for a surprise visit to celebrate my father's eightieth birthday when the news came. So Shirley was the first to visit Donuts and reported back that the head of the department of pediatric cardiology was overseeing her care and that she seemed stable, in good hands, and pretty darned cute.

Finding Donuts made me realize that abandonments are not just statistical events in the long demographic history of China. They happen to real babies who are left in the cold by real people who feel real pain about it, possibly for the rest of their lives. The reality of Donuts, lying in that alleyway alone, refueled my passion to find out more about how babies like her and Grace and Lucy end up on the roadside in the first place.

By then I was beginning to wonder about the creation myth I had always told them—the one I'd been telling since they were toddlers, the parable of the kindly parents and the evil one-child policy that meant they had to give up their children. Maybe that version was true. In the case of Donuts, maybe her parents truly couldn't afford her medical bills. But I knew there were countless other more mundane if equally painful explanations that were just as plausible. Maybe Donuts's parents thought it simply wasn't worth investing in a child who might always be sickly. Maybe they decided to sink that money into a new business or a new iPhone. Maybe they just wanted to try for a perfect child next time.

The range of possibilities for my normal healthy girls was just about as broad. Maybe their mothers were young migrant factory workers who forgot to unroll the condom carefully when taking it off. Maybe they were teen-age schoolgirls, who have been known to throw babies in trash cans even in the richest nations. Maybe my girls were born a few months too soon, violating strict birth-spacing policies. Maybe their mother was a prostitute or a mistress; maybe she was just plain poor. Perhaps their births were sim-ply inconvenient—or maybe they were the greatest tragedies their parents ever experienced. There is even a remote possibility that they were trafficked. Chances are we will never know—about them or about Baby Donuts.

For all of them, their life history begins in an orphanage—not in the bed where they were conceived, or in the hospital where they were born, or in the arms where they first suckled. It begins in an institution. I couldn't visit Grace and Lucy when they were living in their first orphanage homes, but I was determined to get to know everything I could about Donuts's institutional beginnings.

Within weeks of her abandonment, Donuts had been discharged from the hospital and was living at the Shanghai orphanage. Before my first visit, arranged by the Shanghai government, I had prepared myself for a Dickensian experience, with Chinese characteristics. But there was Donuts, just on the other side of a thick glass wall, five months old and smiling in the arms of a buck-toothed orphanage nurse clad in a pink peaked cap and an expression of compassion. By then orphanage staff had estimated her age and used it to assign an official birthdate of October 28, 2010. She was given a name through equally scientific means: Jiang, her surname, was the same as all babies who entered the orphanage in 2010; Xinqian, her first name, a combination of the character *Xin*, given to all orphanage babies inducted in December of that year, and the character *qian*, just for her.

When I got home, Grace was doing what she did every weekday after-noon: slouching in her school uniform sweats multitasking mobile devices on our tattered, dog-chewed sofa, getting up only to replenish the bowl of olive oil and sea salt potato chips or getting the nanny to do it. Old episodes of *Friends* were playing in the background while she worked hard at not doing her math homework. But she sat up in anticipation when she heard I'd been to see Donuts. Luckily, I didn't need to censor anything. "She's in a really cheerful room, and there are lots and lots of other babies with her, and the nannies all seem really nice," I told her.

I was allowed to visit Donuts one more time at the orphanage with its manicured lawns and ostentatiously choreographed flowerbeds, and then my article was published, and as the government saw things, I no longer had any excuse for meddling. So I turned my attention to a new mission: making sure I didn't lose touch with Baby Donuts once she eventually left the orphanage. Until then, I figured the best I could do would be to buy a slice of cake on her fictitious birthday each year to celebrate, just as we did the fictitious birthdays of my own girls. Baby Donuts was the third child I never had, Grace and Lucy's sister in abandonment.

Donuts turned one in the orphanage, and Grace and I shopped around for a slice of birthday cake to celebrate. We settled on a chunk of cream cake from the local Hong Kong confectionary, with its precise layers of vanilla sponge, chocolate frosting, and whipped cream collapsing when she and I attacked it with our forks. (Lucy never held much with sweets.) "Baby Donuts probably doesn't even know it's her birthday," Grace said, and I thought of how seventy-five people had attended my baby's first birthday party, the one with the lurid green dragon cake. I hoped that one day, Donuts would have a mother to waste her time making zodiac cakes.

By then, the Shanghai government had paid for Baby Donuts's heart operation, which left her with one toddler breast plate overlapping the other alarmingly, giving her chest a prow-like appearance. I hadn't seen her since she was a babe in arms. I'd begged the government to let me know who adopted her or tell the new parents how to reach me, but they had refused. Still, a kind lady from the Shanghai foreign affairs office had promised I'd at least be told when Donuts had been adopted. I figured I could trace her then, via adoption agencies overseas that would understand why.

Then, on the eve of her second birthday, the call came: Donuts had been matched with a foreign family. All I needed to figure out was who they were. Crouched over my laptop into the wee hours, neck muscles tense from excitement, I shot e-mails to hundreds of adoption contacts around the globe. "I am trying to find the parents of the baby below, from Shanghai orphanage in China: Jiang Xinqian, dob 10/28/2010, repaired heart defect ASD, recognizable by the large uncorrected lump on her right eye(lid)…I am the person who found her when she was abandoned in the street in Shanghai nearly two years ago. Please help me stay in touch with her."

I got up to stretch and padded down the stairs of our two-up, two-down townhouse, past the tiny bedroom where Grace and Lucy still slept in their toddler bunk beds because that's all the room could accommodate. By the time I'd boiled the kettle, grabbed a pinch of green tea from the canister that never went empty in our fridge, and made it back to my laptop, I had contact details for the new parents. And then, at about 2:00 a.m., this tearjerker landed in my inbox from Donuts's new mommy: "First I need to say that I open my arms wide to the lady that God used to find our daughter and love her first. This gift today is a treasure to me that you cannot imagine! I just cannot believe this: I'm so happy. I would love to sit down and share so much with you about our journey to her." So much for the parents not wanting to know the story of Donuts's finding night.

LaKasha and Jeremy Strickland had stood on street corners near their Louisiana home, holding a bucket and begging for dollar bills, with a grainy picture of a Chinese baby on a poster that said "Bring Baby Bella to America." They didn't have anywhere near the $30,000 that it took to adopt a disabled Chinese foundling. But they had a firm if irrational faith that it could be done. That's how they became Donuts's parents.

I was thrilled and overtired and scared and overemotional finding out about them, but most of all, I am ashamed to say, I felt suspicious. How could a family of impecunious evangelicals—who believed, among other things, that God had deposited miracle funds in their bank account for the adoption—possibly be good enough for my honorary third daughter? What if they couldn't raise the funds to come get her? What if they couldn't support her? What if they were crazy, anyway?

And then seven months later, Donuts was charging across a hotel lobby to meet me in that headlong, stiff-legged way that toddlers too long in an orphanage tend to have, and I was clinging to her new mother LaKasha, speechless with joy to see how LaKasha already loved her.

As stories go, the tale of how Donuts turned into Bella Xin KaLare Strickland of West Monroe, Louisiana was a heart-wrenching one. From Communist tragedy to Christian fairy tale, all in the space of two and a half short years. One minute an abandoned orphan lying in a cold dark alleyway. The next, a feisty toddler, living the life of Barbie in sunny Louisiana. No one could make this stuff up.

I'd never had any trouble understanding why Donuts's birth parents left her in the street. I was less clear on what made LaKasha and Jeremy, living on a shoestring in a town seven thousand miles away with a seven-year-old biological son, wanted to do for Baby Donuts what her own family could or would not do. So I asked them, over bowling and hot pot, while the newly christened Bella napped and threw her toddler tantrums on the one long day we spent together in Shanghai before baby Bella went to America.

Even their US adoption agency had warned them off her, saying the baby had "too many red flags," LaKasha told me, admitting that they had only had $100 in their bank account when this $30,000 journey started. Jeremy had been medically retired from the US Air Force for chronic headaches, and LaKasha had recently quit her job. Adopting a child with major medical needs wasn't the obvious next move.

The Stricklands weren't coy about why they did it: among other reasons, because God wanted them to. And they didn't just make a decision; they mounted a crusade. They set up a tent in the parking lot of the local Walmart to sell T-shirts emblazoned with these words from James 1:27: "Pure and lasting religion in the sight of God our Father is to care for orphans in their troubles." They sold "chicken cheesy spaghetti" lunches to raise $2,500. And they even stood in the street panhandling.

LaKasha said she was shocked at first when Jeremy came up with the idea of standing on street corners. "It was so hard at first, feeling silly and prideful," she wrote. "But after a little wait, a few cars started pulling in and asking about her and putting dollars in our bucket. We got to share about her and about God's love and plan for her life," she said, concluding excitedly "This was ministry! He has given us a way to talk to strangers about him and what he has done and will continue to do. There's nothing easier to talk about than a child in need."

Bella became a member of the family long before she got to Louisiana. On her second birthday (which the baby spent in the orphanage), the Stricklands posed for a family portrait, each clutching a doughnut, to symbolize their bond with the baby of the same nickname. LaKasha even dyed her hair Asian black right before they came to China so that Bella would not be too shocked at her. Still, when the orphanage nanny tried to hand two-and-a-half-year-old Bella over to her new family, she was terrified. The abject misery on her face was captured in the gotcha video (https://www. youtube.com/watch?v=u9mAkXmu8UA). I'm a sucker for handover videos at the best of times, but there was a pain I couldn't imagine ever being healed. How could a child survive what happened to Bella—or to any of our girls?

But by the time I joined the family for a visit scarcely forty-eight hours after that, Bella had already begun to blossom. Fearless, adventuresome, determined, feisty, winsome, and mischievous, she tripped off on her too-spindly legs to explore her surroundings.

Her new family was obviously besotted and pointed out the cataracts in her eyes and the mismatched breast plates like other parents might brag about dimples. What about the prominent bruise in the middle of one cheek? "The orphanage said they weren't sure how that happened," LaKasha told me. Orphanage staff had told the Stricklands that Bella was "very strong willed"—and I don't think they meant it as a compliment.

I gave Bella her first American french fry. I think I saw it as an important bonding ritual. We'd just finished reenacting the scene of her abandonment at the Dunkin Donuts in the company of John Fearon, her official finding person, his grown kids, the new parents, new big brother Peyton, and Bella, the baby on the carrier bags. We'd stared solemnly at the spot, just behind the gate and against the wall, where she'd been deposited. We'd peered through the glass of the Dunkin Donuts, which had since gone out of business. We'd remembered what it was like to go in for a doughnut and come out to find a baby.

Bella had squirmed through all the predictable parental weeping and wailing, the photos, and the exclamations of adults overcome by the tragic miracle that is every Chinese adoption. McDonald's was just around the corner, so we decamped there to recover and to savor the expression of ecstasy on Bella Xin KaLare's face at the taste of her first American cultural experience.

And then we all silently beamed a message to that desperate mother—the one who packed those carrier bags and tied up that bunting—to tell her Bella was going to America and would be just fine. And that we all, every one of us, loved her.

Miracle as it was to meet the new Bella and her new family, it all left me feeling, if anything, even more conflicted about this whole adoption gig. Since Donuts had had her heart operation in the orphanage nearly two years before she was adopted, why did she need to move to Louisiana at all? Couldn't a Chinese family have adopted her? Or for that matter, couldn't she have stayed with her birth family and had her defect repaired by a Chinese charity or by the state? Why did she have to be exported? And where was the morality in exporting my own perfectly healthy daughters?

Soon it was time to drop the newly enlarged Strickland family back at their hotel, cling one last time to LaKasha, and hand over my honorary third daughter to her care forever. The taxi driver wanted to know why LaKasha and I were weeping. So I gave him the potted version of the Donuts-to-Bella saga and threw in by way of explanation that my own daughters were also adopted. As one does in a Chinese taxi, we got chatting about birth parents.

"People who abandon babies are evil," he said, voicing the almost universal Chinese condemnation for the practice. And then he surprised me with this: "Are you afraid they won't love you any more if they find their birth parents?"

And I had to admit that had never occurred to me. I know it's hard for taxi drivers to understand, but we are as deep and as real and as solid a family as was ever created under the sun. Adoption has nothing to do with it. Blood is not always thicker than water.

And that's when he asked the hilarious question without which no taxi journey in China is ever complete: "Do they know they're adopted?" Yes, Bella and Grace and Lucy do all know they are adopted. Oddly enough, they've noticed that they are Chinese, and we, their parents, are not. The more interesting question is, how much do they care?

CHAPTER 10

Child Brides and Abandonment Specialists

"I ABORTED EVERY BABY AFTER the first one," said the middle-aged woman with the broad brown face and improbably straight peasant's teeth. She wouldn't tell me her name, but she was happy to share every detail of her reproductive history. Her first was a son, so every baby after that meant a trip to the local government abortion clinic where the unwanted—nay, illegal—excess child could be cheaply disposed of, as required by the one-child policy.

I'd gone to Jiwang Town, a filthy, muddy, prosperous recycling village on the toxic fringes of the economic miracle that is Shanghai, to interview the city's poor about the country's stock market crash. But when I realized that the woman I was interviewing happened to be from Yangzhou, Grace's hometown, I stopped talking stocks and started picking her brains on my favorite topic: infant abandonment. That's how I ended up perched on a low wooden stool in a shack filled with rusty screws and mismatched washers and slivers of plastic stripped off copper wiring chatting about abortion with a woman who could so easily have been Grace's mother.

Increasingly, this was what I did in my spare time: I went in search, not just of my kids' homeland, but of their whole life stories. I was looking for something I could never have found had they been with me: the reason why they were abandoned in the first place. Even in our no-secrets family, that was information best assembled in private—not just to avoid upsetting the children, but to avoid boring them as well. Throughout their early teen years, they showed precisely zero interest in this topic that had come to fascinate me. They didn't give a hoot about being Chinese, and they didn't give a darn about how they ended up becoming little Americans. But I was determined to keep on giving a damn, on their behalf.

I grilled anyone and everyone I met for little bits of their backstories: my Chinese colleague's electrician happened to hail from near Grace's hometown, so we picked his brain for all he knew; the boss of a steel mill turned out to have been deputy mayor of Lucy's birthplace when she was a baby; by the end of our chat, he was offering to try to help find her birth parents. With masseuses and hairdressers, pedicurists and other people's maids, I chatted abandonment trends. While my horny old toenails soaked in a basin of rose-strewn water, I'd talked abortion practices with migrant nail artists happy to find anyone who cared what it was like back home. Lying face down on the grimy taffeta-skirted massage table while my favorite massage torturer dug her elbows into my ancient Chinese pressure points, I'd bark out a question or two between grunts and moans. How many kids do you have? Did you abort any? Abandon any? Worse? Gender selection had been a fact of life in China for hundreds of years by the time I got there; nobody was coy about it.

That's how I ended up interrogating Grace's Yangzhou kinswoman about the intimate indignities of the one-child policy. "The peak period for abandoning babies was 1989 to 1999," she mused, not knowing how my heart thrilled to hear that last date, the year that Yang Shu Min was born. "Most of the abandoned babies were girls whose parents wanted to have a boy but wanted to avoid the huge punishment for having more than one child," she recalled, without either shame or condemnation, almost bored. She herself would have faced a fine of as much as $10,000 for each surplus child—several years' earnings for a woman like her. No sane person would have done otherwise, she seemed to say; the area where she and Grace were born enforced the one-child policy so strictly that rural families weren't even allowed to try for a boy if the first one was a girl, as they often were in other areas.

I was fighting tears as she talked; this might be the closest I would ever get to Grace's life story. Everything about that unseasonably hot spring day is etched in my memory. The way her husband squatted beside her, meticulously sifting nuts, bolts, washers, and bits of wire to glean even the tiniest bit to sell as scrap. The way toxic dust clung to every surface in the room, from the bed covered by makeshift mosquito netting in the corner to the rice cooker on the shelf and the hands of the toddler grandson who waddled into the room and peed through his split-trousered overalls on the floor. The way no one seemed to notice.

The woman was warming to the task of helping me speculate on Grace and her antecedents: "Abandoned children usually have an elder sister and a younger brother," she said, unwittingly confirming what I had always told Grace—that she most likely has siblings in exactly that order. "Young women who get pregnant before marriage would also discard their children, usually within a few days after birth, because after that, the mother would get attached and not want to give her child away. The usual way to dump a child was either to give it to a childless couple or put in on the roadside where there are people passing by," she said. It sounded so rational; they could choose door number one or door number two. Grace's parents clearly chose door number two.

She was quick to assure me that, in their shared hometown, things didn't happen that way in 2015, when I was visiting her. "Now, villagers don't dump their healthy girls. If you give birth to two daughters now, you have two daughters." In other words, if Grace had been born later, she wouldn't be my daughter. What began as just a routine day's work for the *Financial Times* had yielded insights beyond measure—not to mention a reminder of what a remarkable accident of fate, politics, and economics made us a family in the first place.

On her part, it was all strangely unemotional: forced abortion was a fact of life, abandonment was what any sane person would do, and adoption was a win-win solution. The people of Yangzhou did what they had to do (abort or abandon), and I did what I had to do (adopt). Surely nobody could be blamed for any of that, could they?

Only slowly did it dawn on me that I was forgetting one important variable in the equation of one-child policy = families that can't afford to keep girls = perfect solution of international adoption: money. Cash greased the wheels of even the most legitimate foreign adoption from China. And I'd been acting like it all happened for free.

The young woman in the stone-washed jeans and too-tight white lace top always knew she was destined to marry her brother—she just didn't know there was anything unusual about that.

Talk about unintended consequences of the one-child policy. Born in 1983, a few years after the introduction of the policy in 1979, she was sold by her birth parents, who could not afford an extra girl, to a baby broker, who resold her to a family that needed a wife for their son. "My parents bought me for two hundred sixty renminbi," (about a hundred dollars back then), she said, referring to the family that raised her from infancy. "I was a bit expensive," she said, blushing with pride. "My parents borrowed that money to save me. They needed to pay relatives back for that money, so I felt grateful."

I'd spent years pretending that what I had done was nothing like what had happened to this woman. Sure, I'd raided my bank balance to bring someone else's child into my home, just like the people who bought her did. But I'd had no choice, right? To adopt a Chinese child, non-Chinese adoptive parents had to pay a compulsory donation to the orphanage ($3,000 when I adopted Grace and Lucy, later raised to $5,000). It was couched as compensation for the care offered. While I knew Grace could never have drunk $3,000 worth of baby formula in her eight months in state custody, I reassured myself that the excess had gone to improving care for the babies left behind. I wasn't trafficking, I told myself. I was subsidizing the Chinese orphanage system. And I told other adoptive parents—some of them wracked with guilt about the mandatory donations—exactly the same thing. Handing over money for a child bride is trafficking; handing over money for a legally acquired child is different, isn't it?

Still, facing this child bride at a chipped and greasy Formica table in a working man's diner in Lucy's home province of Anhui, I was no longer so sure. The people who bought her were not evil; they just needed a bride for their son. I wasn't evil, either. I wanted babies for my life. But arguably, we were all traffickers. We all parted with cash to get our kids. That's not the story I'd told myself before I started poking around, looking for the real China, and it certainly wasn't the story I told my kids. But the black-and-white morality of it all had begun to blur for me. Somehow, the mental image of those 260 crumpled one-renminbi notes, infused with the sweat and soil of the peasant parents who sold her, and the jumble of small light coins that marked her worth finally made me face a truth I'd always avoided: in China, adoption is always, on some level, all about the money.

Chinese birth parents give up babies because the state won't let them keep them, and adoptive parents fork out for the privilege of stepping in. Whether it's a pile of coins handed over in the dead of night to buy a child bride or an envelope bulging with stiff Mao-faced notes handed over to an orphanage director, there's always a financial transaction involved. At the end of the day, on some level, it's all trafficking. With her gratitude and her pride and her shame, this woman had finally made me see that.

Not that she was complaining. The twenty-something young woman insisted that she was devoted to the family that bought her. Marrying their son was the least she could do for them "My parents treated me very well," she protested. "If I was starving, and there was only one bowl of rice left, I would give it to my mother," she said, referring to the woman who bought her as "Ma."

Ma told her that the family adopted her because they wanted a daughter. But in the small village in Fujian province where she grew up and where many of her friends were also child brides—four within the extended family—everyone knew the score. They were purchased for procreation.

And not just any kind of procreation. The goal was to produce a son and heir, and nothing less would do. So when she bore a daughter at eighteen years old, she was pressured to stop nursing so she could conceive again immediately. Not until she had a son did the family formalize her union with a marriage license, procured with a sixty-dollar bribe to a local official since, as a trafficked infant, she didn't have any identity papers. When an *FT* colleague and I interviewed her, the children were nine and eleven and asking awkward questions like "Why is your mother the same as Dad's?"

Tall and slender, with sleek hair side parted to fall fetchingly over one eye, she was in the prime of life and stuck with two kids in a marriage she was sold into. She could get out but only if she agreed to leave the son of the union behind and take along the daughter, whom her in-laws had no use for. Too soon, Ma had tracked her down—she wasn't normally allowed out of the house—and shown up at the greasy spoon with both kids in tow, and the interview came to an end. And the sister-spouse went back to her brother-husband, back to the quasi bondage that her parents sold her into so long ago.

I was left with a heart heavier all the time at the thought that any child over whom money changes hands has effectively been trafficked. I'd started to lose my footing on the moral high ground that had always underpinned our family: that I did a good deed to adopt them. I'd gone out to look for my girls' homeland and their backstories, and what I'd come up with instead were doubts about whether they should even be my children.

But wait a minute. Was there any chance that the money trail was even more sordid than that? Could my children actually have been sold to the orphanage? A baby-selling ring had been busted in China's Hunan province soon after we arrived in China. It involved brokers selling babies to orphanage directors for a fraction of the compulsory donation from adoptive parents ($5,000 by then); directors bought babies to place for overseas adoption and pocketed the profit. I'd always told myself that practice hadn't become common until long after my girls were adopted and then only by a handful of dirty orphanages—not by the "better" orphanages that my kids came from. But over time, that rationalization lost its comfort for me. I wanted to know what had actually happened to them. Was there any chance that, just like that bride for hire, their parents voluntarily sold them into the home of a stranger?

The middle-aged electrician had the wiry build of those undernourished as children and the stained teeth of those prosperous enough to splurge on smokes as adults. He was afraid of me, probably just because I was a foreigner. I doubt it had anything to do with the patently illegal activities we were about to discuss.

My *FT* colleague and dear friend Shirley (Shasha) Chen had discovered this guy while he was rewiring her apartment. She was a bit like me back then; if anyone admitted to hailing from Yangzhou, she would delve straight into his or her personal fertility database. With the electrician, she unearthed something extraordinary: the mousy little guy with his head inside the wall had spent his childhood following around his family's abandonment specialist. He was exactly the kind of person I needed to give me a nuts-and-bolts primer on abandonment. After all, he was actually there when several unwanted girls were, in the most humane way possible, discarded.

The Jiwang trash picker had told the tale from the point of view of one of the mothers of Yangzhou. But they weren't always (or even very often) the ones who made the decision about what to do with excess babies. That decision often fell to the matriarch of the family, the maternal grandmother, keeper of traditional values and fierce guardian of the bloodline. And to help her out with that, extended families often designated one senior relative as the family's abandonment expert. Here before me was a relative who had followed him around, perhaps as a kind of understudy.

He talked and smoked and smoked and talked—and shouted into the phone in an unintelligible local dialect when he wanted to check a detail—for two hours. "Abandoning kids was done in a very sophisticated way. If the family made up their minds to abandon a baby, at least three to five relatives would go around investigating if there was another family who wanted a baby and could afford to raise it. They'd discuss the feasibility and the timing and a good place to abandon the baby. They always wanted to find a good family," he was at pains to reassure us. He was a child back then, but what he remembered was the grief: "The [birth] mother might keep on weeping for a week."

The man hardly lifted his chopsticks, so intense was the mental effort it took to calculate how many babies had been dealt with in this way. He made a phone call back home at one point, bellowing to make sure his query made it all the way to the village, and finally came up with a tally of twenty in one family. At least twenty of his close relatives either abandoned female infants or adopted them during his childhood. So this was a fairly commonplace occurrence. "No orphanage could take those babies. So they would take them to the police station, and a female member of the family would stay nearby until someone went to ask about adopting the baby. Only if no one came for three days, the police would give the child back."

141

What happened then was left unspecified, perhaps deliberately. "Two of my female cousins were adopted, and my wife's female cousin was also adopted," he said. But girls adopted that way did not always forgive those who had abandoned them, even if they had no choice. "My aunt abandoned a girl at a relative's who was wealthier...When the girl grew to be thirteen or fourteen, the biological parents wanted to visit her, but the girl beat them every time she saw them, and when she got married, her birth parents weren't able to see her."

His tone was flat, but his empathy was deep. Sometimes discarded girls never forgave their parents. "One father found out that the girl he abandoned was not happy in the adoptive family, so he knelt down at the front gate of that family every day begging them to give the girl back and offering to pay twenty or thirty times the cost of raising her, just to get her back," he recalled. "Usually such kids are not willing to go back to their biological parents, but when they become mothers themselves, they sometimes accept their birth mother as a kind of aunt," he explained.

By that point in the conversation, I really wanted to know more about exactly how all this was done. I'd been on the receiving end of an abandonment, but he was in on the planning stages. "They usually didn't abandon the girl until she was twenty to thirty days old. First, other family members would go to make sure that the [targeted] family would adopt her. Then they'd wrap her to make her warm and safe from animal attack." That's a detail I could have done without, imagining my own girls by the side of a Chinese road, with beady predator eyes sizing them up.

"Maybe they'd put her in a barn in the hay at two or three in the morning, when people would easily wake up. When the go-between put the baby down, he would make noise to raise the alarm and then wait hidden nearby until he saw a light from their window and someone open the door and take the girl inside. The other family members would be waiting at home for the go-between to bring the news that the girl had been accepted by the family, and only then did they feel the situation was secure. They usually placed a bottle of milk with the baby, too, because they knew the adoptive family would not be prepared." My mind leaped to the image of a sleepy farmer, stumbling to the barn to investigate the commotion and coming back to his barren wife in their warm bed with a baby swaddled in his arms. I think I know how she felt.

And to make sure they could prove she was theirs, even years down the line, "Most people put a token inside the baby's wrapping" he said.

He didn't say what the token was, but Yangzhou girl Lily Mueller had such a parental note written on rice paper in her bunting, according to her mother, Tonia: "I'm told my daughter's letter was beautifully written. It said that the mother was presenting her precious baby because she was unable to keep her, that she loved her very much and begged the finder to find a mother for her who would love her as much, too. And she wrote that she would kowtow every day of her life to that mother who would always love her daughter. She expressed her pain and gave the date of the baby's birth. I really wanted to keep the original, but the orphanage said I could only have a copy."

"At that time we didn't have DNA tests, so if you wanted to find your child later, you had to rely on such tokens, which usually showed the date the child was born and maybe included some clothing." The electrician picked up the thread. He stressed yet again that he thought all this was "a very responsible way to abandon babies."

But he was adamant that by the time Grace came along, it was far from routine to abandon girls that way. That was not exactly the news I wanted to hear. If most people didn't discard babies by then, then why was Grace thrown away? Was there any chance her parents sold her—if not to another family, then to an orphanage that could turn her around for a profit? I didn't dare ask, so instead I grilled him desperately for alternative explanations. Anything to defend the morality of adopting her.

He couldn't remember exactly when abandonment had become rare, but he was certain of why. Previously, parents who had too many kids faced having their house torn down, the husband and even grandfather brutally beaten. Even paying the impossibly steep fine was not enough; local officials wanted parents bearing excess children to suffer.

But he said that the policy was eventually relaxed to allow second births, if the first was a girl—and sometimes even if it wasn't. (The policy was relaxed again in October 2015 to allow all Chinese parents to have two children.) The rising tide of Chinese affluence meant more and more Yangzhou area parents could afford the extra-baby fine of about six hundred dollars, and the government would even take an IOU. In his view, any child under twenty could not have been abandoned because of the one-child policy; there were plenty of ways around it by then.

It seemed like he might be flirting with the conclusion that I urgently willed him not to reach: baby selling. But that never seemed to have occurred to him. "She must be the child of parents who were not married," he concluded firmly. "Maybe the mother was just an innocent girl herself." Back to square one. Who knew why Grace was abandoned? Was it because of the one-child policy—or in spite of it?

Lucky for me, I soon discovered that I was not the only mother of an adopted Chinese child wandering around the rural Chinese countryside asking nosy questions about why people gave up their babies. I found someone else who'd been doing it for two decades, mostly in the province where Lucy was born. It was time to start poking into Lucy's life story.

Jiang Shengshi was born at almost exactly the same time as Fu Xinke, my Lucy, and in the same part of China. Both were adopted by Americans. Both were born in tragedy. The only difference between them was that Shengshi's birth parents told the terrible tale of her beginnings. Maybe one day Lucy's will do the same. Until then, I must rely on what Shengshi's parents told Kay Johnson, that other adoptive mother rattling around in the Chinese countryside reading the tea leaves of her child's abandonment.

For her book *China's Hidden Children: Abandonment, Adoption, and the Human Costs of the One-Child Policy*, she and her colleagues interviewed 350 parents who abandoned infants, 1,000 Chinese families who adopted domestically (often informally), and 800 who hid children to avoid stiff fines, forced sterilization, or even confiscation of the child. She found that, like Shengshi's parents, many risked life, limb, and penury for a daughter.

But wait a minute. Chinese people hate girls, right? Surely that's why my kids were abandoned. Even random strangers in Walmart used to trot out that bit of global conventional wisdom in front of my girls when they were toddlers in the shopping cart. "Isn't it awful how they treat girls over there?" they would ask while giving my cuties a sweet. Thank God there were good Christian families in America ready to scoop up the discarded daughters of China. I usually didn't bother telling them I wasn't a Christian, but I certainly did tell them—not least because my children were listening—that Chinese people don't despise daughters.

The story of Shengshi, whose name means *victory*, is a case in point. She was the illegal second daughter of a rural family that already had a son. The mother fervently wanted a daughter, so she hid the pregnancy, threatening her health and that of the fetus by keeping as thin as possible. She and her husband took turns watching the baby indoors until she was nine months old, when birth control bureaucrats discovered her anyway. She ended up in an overseas adoption.

And one day, her foreign parents heard the story of how all this had happened from Shengshi's own birth father. It was any adoptive parents' worst nightmare: their child was born of love, hidden at risk of physical injury, and torn from the grieving arms of her birth parents when all else failed to keep her. She was not, as most of us foreign parents liked to think, given up voluntarily—if you can call being forced to give up a child by a government policy "voluntary." There was no lack of love in the home she came from.

Could Grace and Lucy be like her? Were they really abandoned by the side of the road only hours after birth? Or were they cherished by parents or adoptive parents for weeks or months and only later torn from their arms to be sent overseas? Ms. Johnson's book gave me pause.

Sure, Chinese peasants had been drowning extra daughters since time immemorial. Agrarian cultures needed sons, and Asian cultures needed men to extend the bloodline; daughters became part of the husband's household and were often not even recorded in family lineage records. Chinese peasants used illegal sex-selective abortions to choose boys for the same reasons. But the point was, when they had a choice, Chinese proved really quite partial to girls. And getting more partial all the time: the sex ratio at birth, which was more than 120:100 when we got to China in 2008, had declined by 2015 to less than 113:100 and is falling. China would soon be no more misogynistic than the rest of us.

So far, so comforting, but Ms. Johnson's other conclusions were far harder to stomach. She found that a lot of the excess daughters of China were not, as I had always believed, abandoned by their birth parents and taken straight to the orphanage. Many were first placed informally in childless or daughterless homes carefully vetted by their birth parents. Even so, at least a dozen such infants in her small sample ended up overseas.

What? So there was not, as I had always been told, a shortage of local families willing and able to adopt? No cultural reluctance to adopt girls or even to adopt at all? On the contrary, Ms. Johnson argued, only the government was reluctant. Beijing didn't want extra babies ending up in local adoptive homes because it didn't want that hungry mouth to have existed in the first place. Allowing local adoption would have defeated the whole purpose of the one-child policy; the Communist Party wasn't going to permit such an obvious loophole.

And that's where I came into it. By shipping babies like Grace and Lucy out of the country, Beijing found homes for them without blurring the party line on birth control. That meant foreign adoption was, effectively, a tool of one-child policy enforcement. And Ms. Johnson wasn't going to let me pretend otherwise.

It wasn't my fault. I know that intellectually. But the more I read her book and the more trash pickers and electricians and child brides I talked to, the more I wondered about my own complicity in what happened. And yes, I know the ultimate cause was the policy itself: the Communist Party's grand plan for guaranteeing Chinese prosperity by getting a handle on the population explosion in a way that countries like democratic but impoverished India could never have done. But Ms. Johnson wanted me to face the fact that people like me (and her) were among the clearest beneficiaries of a policy that included everything from beatings to mandatory sterilizations, forced abortions, and penalties as high as ten times annual household income.

Birth parents lost children they might have fervently wanted to keep; childless Chinese couples lost the chance to adopt a child of their own ethnicity; my children lost the love of the people who conceived them, loved them first, and may grieve for them forever—and the right to grow up among people who look like them. They will never take their rightful place in one of the oldest cultures on earth. And I got two healthy, lovely, talented daughters I could never have had any other way. Ms. Johnson made me face the fact that others suffered so I could reap that windfall.

The standard for adoptions around the world is that babies should be voluntarily relinquished. Could that ever be said to have happened in China? Grace and Lucy were adopted legally—at least the US and Chinese governments certified that they were—but where was the morality in it? That's a lot less clear to me than it used to be.

Then Beijing cast aside the one-child policy altogether in October 2015, and I wondered whether it was ever necessary in the first place. Some Chinese demographers think it was based on a mistake tallying up the statistics. They say the high birth rate that frightened the Communist Party into adopting it nationwide in 1979 had been halved even before it took effect, but Beijing didn't notice the downward trend. So I gained daughters from a brutal policy that was completely unnecessary. I'm not sure how I feel about that.

When news of the abolition came out in the form of a one-line tweet from the state Xinhua news agency at dinnertime one fall day, I shouted down the stairs to Grace, then planning her sixteenth birthday party, "There's no more one-child policy!" It didn't escape me that, had the policy been abolished sixteen years earlier, I wouldn't even have a daughter to celebrate a birthday with.

She was thrilled, or as thrilled as a child can be with sweet sixteen on her mind. "Wow, that's amazing," she shouted back, without taking her eyes off the group chat planning her birthday trip to the local escape room, where she would be forced to solve riddles and puzzles with friends in Chinese to get out of a locked room. And that's what I found the most comforting of all: the fact that Grace refused to give two thoughts to the circumstances of her birth, to the abandonment she had known about since a toddler, or to the way we became a family. It all simply bored her. Including the Chineseness part.

CHAPTER 11

The Amazing Gene Race

"Mom, Dad, I want to find you." Yang Renci had rehearsed this simple phrase in her sweet-toned schoolgirl Mandarin, and she pronounced it precisely on the evening news in Yangzhou, the hometown she shared with Grace. Ren, as she was known in English, had come looking for her birth parents, just to let them know that she was fine.

Ren was part of our Yangzhou extended family, even if, several years older than Grace, she never shared a crib with her. They shared the next best thing: a sweet unselfish desire to ease the pain of a birth mother who might not otherwise even know her child was still alive.

"I just want to know how they are doing, make sure they know I'm OK," seventeen-year-old Ren told us all over a plate of the people's food, Shanghainese crispy soup dumplings, right before leaving to look for her biological parents. Would she be angry if she found out they gave her up to try for a boy? "It's not their fault. Society has created a culture where boys are more favored. I wouldn't blame them," she said, between slurps.

"What if they need money?" I asked, not willing to admit that had always been one my biggest fears. What if birth grandma needed a heart transplant? I'd always blown hot and cold on the topic of birth-parent searching. I desperately wanted to know the why of my kids' background, but I feared the emotional, the moral, and, yes, the financial entanglements all that could bring.

But Ren was scarcely more than a child herself, so I guess none of that had occurred to her. "A part of me would have that instinct, to owe them. I would definitely want to help them." I didn't ask whether that meant she was ready to drain her college fund to help, though that's what I really wanted to know.

I never lost any sleep worrying that my children would choose their birth parents over me, even in the remote event that they could find them. As teens, they weren't all that keen on me, but odds were they wouldn't like Chinese birth parents much better. It was parents, of whatever ethnicity, they saw no point in.

So I was never much given to angst over losing my children's love. It was their money I was worried about. That new heart for Grandma, dialysis for Mom's cousin twice removed, a nursing home for Granddad, college for the son they gave up my daughter to conceive: finding birth parents could bankrupt me, I feared. I was definitely in the minority on this. The tiny minority of adoptive parents who search for and find their kids' biological relatives often feel no obligation to maintain an ongoing relationship with them—and certainly no responsibility to support them financially. But I couldn't bear the thought of tearing my children away from their birth mothers twice. If we do find Grace and Lucy's relatives while I'm still in charge, I will feel the same duty to them as to any of my own biological relatives.

And what if we discovered that more than the statutory amount of money changed hands to facilitate their adoption? If there was trafficking involved—as there surely was in at least a minority of Chinese adoptions—where would that leave me, morally? Most searching families didn't seem to worry about any of this. They were willing to take a leap into the moral and financial unknown, a kind of leap I could never contemplate with alacrity.

And none of that seemed to be troubling Ren. She popped up on Yangzhou television a few days later, appealing for her birth parents to step forward. The results were immediate. Within minutes, an old lady dialed in to the station, claiming, "I know who abandoned her. I know who sent her away. She was taken to [the] orphanage by the toy factory women's association director. I also know who abandoned her. It's my relative, my niece's family."

The frantic family rushed to Ren's hotel where a television crew peppered them with questions.

"Why did you give her up?"

"Do you think she looks like [you]?"

Right away, their hopes began to unravel. "We were hiding in a small house outside to give birth to the baby. It was just a few days after she was born that we wrapped her and sent her away. If the village knew, we would be fined," explained the grieving mother. But Ren was already six months old when she was brought to the orphanage, and she wasn't found by a toy factory official.

The family decided the orphanage records must be wrong; this had to be their daughter. "I think her eyes are like my mother's," said the putative birth family's son—the very son they gave up a daughter to conceive. An aunt insisted that Ren looked like the mother. But it was soon clear that Ren could not be their child. An elder daughter wondered if her mother would be able to bear the disappointment.

That scenario was repeated again and again while we were in China. Adoptees would come to the motherland on the gene hunt and then unearth several sets of parents who were not their own—but certainly were somebody else's. Grieving parents who abandoned babies, sometimes decades ago, turned up in multiples, hoping to be reunited with a discarded daughter, even when the dates and details didn't match, and the birth defects didn't align. They wanted to find a lost daughter just by willing it so.

Jenna Cook, an American adoptee, turned up no fewer than forty-four sets of parents claiming to be hers when she came searching for her antecedents in China. And before anyone concludes that they were just trying to hitchhike on her American gravy train, none of the parents wanted anything from her except the miracle of her turning out to be their daughter. One family tried to ply her with a large sum of money, even after they knew they were not related because it was the next best thing to giving it to their own flesh and blood. Maybe Grace or Lucy will reunite with her birth parents that way one day: not because they are looking for parents but because the parents are looking for lost children.

The topic of ancestors was always a touchy one in our family, but not for the reason one might think. As early as kindergarten, teachers introduced my kids to the concept of a family tree, without ever realizing, apparently, that they didn't have one.

That's how Grace found herself, one spring day right before we moved to China, wandering among gravestones soft like bars of soap, their edges worn away by decades of forgetting. The vast expanse of Arlington Cemetery seemed empty, except for one Chinese child who had come to visit her great-great-great grandfather by adoption.

8917. Wm. Waldmeyer. PA. Grace traced the raised letters on the white granite headstone of her earliest known legal relative, Swiss immigrant William Waldmeyer. He died in the American Civil War, serving with a company of Pennsylvania volunteers who fought at the Battle of Gettysburg. (Back then, America was more relaxed about spelling surnames.)

Visiting ancestors' graves is something Chinese people do religiously once a year, but Grace wasn't there out of any sudden attack of filial piety. She had braved a morbid fear of graveyards and the spongy sensation of the turf around the grave ("Yuck! I feel like I can sink right in as far as the casket.") because she needed old Bill to help her solve an existential crisis. Her teacher had had the bright idea that the class should do a family tree, but Grace's tree has no branches. Civil War Bill could help her at least fake one.

All their lives, Grace and Lucy had insisted they couldn't care less that they were adopted, but they did care that they didn't have a dad. And never more so than when some well-intentioned teacher handed out family trees with a thick trunk split down the middle, with one branch just for dad. Even children of divorce have a father, the teacher doubtless told herself. But where other kids had genes, mine had a total void. I could create a fictional maternal bloodline, but who could we get to do daddy duty? That was the kind of practical skill they should have taught us back in adoption parenting school. Forget the grieving, how do you fake a family tree convincingly?

So we dug up some paper ancestors instead. Grace posed for a happy snap with her nineteenth-century forebear by adoption and then pasted it proudly at the very top of her tree. No one else had a Civil War hero at the top of her ancestral chart, even if they did have dads. Whoever said blood was thicker than adoption paperwork?

But faking ancestors won't work forever. As my kids' generation of adopted Chinese children reaches maturity in parallel with the growth of genetic medicine, many want more than genealogies full of people they don't share a drop of blood with. They want a family history of genetic ailments that only a biological parent can provide; they want to know which grandparent gave them their nose and which sibling they most resemble; some want to fill a hole they think only a birth parent can heal. Very few find what they are looking for, but what they discover is, if anything, even more surprising.

Ricki "Mengting" Mudd wasn't six days old like Grace or six months old like Ren when she was separated from her birth parents; she was old enough to have a hazy memory of life before adoption. And this all-American girl was unusual in other ways, too. Unlike the vast majority of the lost daughters of China, she managed to find her birth family and hear her extraordinary story from their lips—in fact, several different versions of it.

"We never intended to abandon her. When we went outside, we would put our child in a big bag with one of us holding both her hands and the other holding her feet so no one would know what was inside," Xu Xianzhen, Ricki's biological mother, said. She had the same broad face and nose as Mengting, the child she last saw as a toddler. She had not forgotten the awkward weight of her end of the sack and the fear that the hidden child would squirm or kick and give away their secret.

"Mengting was such an adorable child, so cooperative. We asked her not to make any noise, and she would stay quiet. At home she would hide upstairs, and be very quiet. We had to keep hiding." Ms. Xu told her story in *Ricki's Promise*, from documentary filmmaker Changfu Chang, who has done some of the best original work on what happens when adopted girls search for biological relations in China.

Biological father Wu Jincai chimed in. "At that time it was terrifying to have an over-quota child. If the government knew about it, you could be in trouble. People would come to your house, remove all your grain, do anything they could to you. Sometimes they'd destroy your house."

Ricki picked up the tale, and things started not adding up. Her parents worked out a deal with a village woman referred to as "Madam Fan," paying her to arrange for an unmarried brother to pose as her adoptive father. "But they didn't keep their promise. After living with them for only a hundred days, I was seized by birth-planning officials," said Ricki. Her birth father tried to steal her back from the orphanage, but he was chased away by staff.

Eventually, after her American adoptive parents were told yet another version of the truth—that Ricki was abandoned at a train station at age seven months—Mengting became Ricki, at nearly five years old. "Ricki was a very angry little girl. She would spit her food on the floor; she would bite; she was very obnoxious. Her behavior was very bad. It was so bad, we thought we might have to take her back to the orphanage and not go through with the adoption," Ricki's adoptive father said on camera, an unusually candid admission for an adoptive parent.

And then one day, the Mudd family got a letter from Madam Fan, pretending to be Ricki's biological grandmother and demanding $10,000. Ricki's true biological parents got wind of Madam Fan's scam and went to her, demanding information about their daughter. A Fan relative slipped them an envelope bearing the American family's return address, and the two families arranged for Ricki to come to China. And then began another period of elaborate subterfuge. Ricki's parents, long divorced, pretended to be living together during her visit and worked hard to create the fiction of a happy reunited family, which included a teenage brother whom they had risked Mengting's safety to bear.

Ricki's reunion with the treacherous Madam Fan was gut wrenching. She had a hazy memory of eating chicken bones off Madam Fan's floor, and she tactfully asked, "Maybe times were hard for you. Was that all I could eat at the time?" Madam Fan, all flattery and obsequiousness for the camera, made no reply.

And other things didn't add up. "I began to wonder if I will ever get a clear answer to what happened in the past," Ricki told the camera. Then she discovered that her birth parents' façade of matrimonial bliss was a fiction, too. In fact, Ricki's birth mother had stabbed the father after she was lost, blaming the paternal grandmother for pressuring the couple for a son. And even worse, the birth mother had never forgiven the son for his unwitting role in the loss of her daughter.

"I'm concerned about my mother's explosive temper, I'm not used to people just smacking a child...she hits Chao [the brother]. She lifted up a chair, and I said, 'What are you doing? He could go to hospital,'" said Ricki. Talk about culture shock: "Those kind of things are very shocking to me. What happens if I don't listen...Will she hit me? That's a normal part of Chinese culture. In China it's OK to hit your kids, but in America if you hit your kids, the government will take them away. I told her if she hit me, I would leave China immediately and take the first flight back to America."

Stories like this put me off the whole idea of a genetic expedition. In a complex culture like China, truth is always just that little bit relative.

Sometimes, a roots search can land adoptive families in situations that are way beyond their comprehension. Another family profiled by Mr. Chang ended up shelling out a considerable sum of money after locating the birth parents of their adopted daughter, the birth family's third girl. The family went on to have a fourth girl, for whom the foreign family paid the excess birth fine, and eventually had a boy, financed by the adoptive family—all to make the birth family's dream of bearing a son come true. And then after all that, one of the birth siblings tried to get yet more money out of the foreign family, telling them a tall tale about the family homestead burning down. Luckily, a savvy translator pulled the plug on that one.

But I was worried less about an outright scam like that—I think such cases are rare—than about having a moral obligation toward people who share my children's bloodline. Ricki worried about that, too. "I want to help out, regardless of obligation," she once told me in an e-mail exchange. "Family is family, and you help out your family, it's as simple as that for me. I also plan on helping out my adoptive parents. I want to be a wonderful daughter to both sets of parents because I love them, and this is my ultimate drive for many of the things I do in life."

"Hey, guys, look at what this girl says about wanting to help out both her birth parents and her adoptive parents. She's the one I told you about, the one who found her biological parents, but it turns out the mother stabbed the father and then pretended to be married to him and then she went mad and she beat the brother and—"

"Mom, we don't wanna to hear about it. Blah Blah Blah. Who cares?" I had been shouting down the stairs to Grace and Lucy, who sat in the living room watching *American Idol* by satellite from the Philippines. I was watching the same show upstairs in my room, since they felt the sitting room couch was too crowded for Mom, what with both of them stretched out full length and our two Chinese street dogs cuddled up on it, too.

So I shouted down the stairs if one of my *Idol* favorites sang a particularly good ballad, and if they didn't shout back, I'd sometimes text them on their iPhones. That sometimes got a response. But not on birth parent search issues. They'd never been able to understand why I had any interest in the topic. Starting a conversation about the birth parents of a girl they didn't even know? "We have to look after you when you're old, Mom. Why would we want to look after anybody else? Stop bothering us and get yourself a dish of ice cream," said Lucy, only half in jest.

And sometimes the story was not quite so pretty as that told by Mengting's mother. It's a rare family that struggles to keep their child as mightily as Mengting's did. Human motives are messy—in China or anywhere else—and not every sob story is created equal. Not every searching child will unearth a fairy tale.

But it was apparent, even to me, that what mattered was not what I thought about all this, but what Grace and Lucy thought. So I put a diary reminder in my calendar to ask them about it, and once a year, on the same date, I asked them.

"Got no time for that," Lucy said at age fourteen in her best vernacular voice, the one she'd learned from years of watching American television ricocheted off a satellite in Manila. Striding loose limbed and skinny jeaned down one of Shanghai's trendiest streets, Lucy was making clear just how sick and tired she was of the annual query about whether she wanted to find her birth parents.

We were taking one of our frequent luxury staycation breaks. My own answer to the problem of getting teens to talk to you: bribe them with a night in a luxury hotel. We'd had back-to-back nights at the landmark art deco Peace Hotel on the Shanghai Bund with a chaser of Waldorf Astoria, with its best-in-Shanghai view of the city's triptych of neon-lit skyscrapers.

I thought I'd outdone myself that time with the accommodations, but even a pillowtop mattress and a flat-screen TV the width of half the hotel room weren't enough to get Lucy interested in this old topic. As usual, she was all pragmatism: "Not now, not at this crucial point in my life," by which she meant when she was trying to prepare applications for college still four long years away. "It just doesn't fit into my plan. I can't take the risk that meeting them will be a really deeply unsettling experience. They might be really different than the image I have in my mind. And it's not a short-term thing. It's forever. I might look after college when I have time," she allowed.

And if it was too late by then? I tentatively inquired; that was why I had started wondering about searching in the first place, because of the fear that if we left it too long, all evidence linking them to their biological families would have disappeared.

"They might be dead by then, but it wouldn't matter since they are dead to me now anyway." I didn't know if she meant that or was just trying to shock me. Only a foolish parent kids herself that she really knows how her teen is feeling.

Grace, as usual, tried to deflect the conversation with the trademark half grin that said she thought Mom and Lucy were unutterably boring. "I like being the eldest in the family, and I don't want to give that place up, since I probably have an older birth sister," said. "Just another sister to hate," she added, proving yet again that teasing Mom was still one of her favorite pastimes. Her responses to the birth parent query were always designed primarily to shut me up. Sometimes she'd say she wanted to reassure bio mom that she was healthy and happy; sometimes she'd say she didn't want to. Her only consistent response, from toddlerhood to adulthood, was "This is boring."

Then Lucy surprised me by bringing up heredity in a way I had not yet even imagined: as it related, not to her parents, but to her children. "I'm definitely having kids. And they're definitely not going to be adopted," she blurted out as we were turning in to the DVD store to pick up two-dollar bootleg copies of Oscar nominating tapes, as one did on a Saturday night in Shanghai. It was the day after Christmas, so the shop's narrow aisles were crammed with expats who, I imagined, were all hanging on her every word.

"Why not?" I tried to keep my tone neutral, though my heart was shrieking, "I'm a failure. She thinks adoption is awful."

But Lucy made clear that, like almost everything in her life as a teen, this had nothing to do with me. "Because I want my DNA to live on. I want that little bit of me to live on in the world, and if I don't have my own kids, that won't happen." Her deep black eyes were, for once, looking straight into mine; for once, she wasn't joking.

"But I feel like a little bit of me lives on in you," I bleated pitifully.

Lucy was not having it. "It's a DNA thing, Mom. You got to spread yo' genes, man," she said, slipping back into television sitcom-speak. "That's why you live. You don't live just so you can die; you live to produce another one of *you*—and then you die."

I comforted myself by thinking this sounded more like a regurgitated biology lesson than an indictment of my parenting.

But Lucy wasn't finished yet. "Or I might adopt, but I'd adopt a baby that looks like me." That couldn't have come from her biology textbook; it had to come straight from the heart.

"Does it bother you, not looking like me?" I asked, not sure I wanted to know the answer.

"Watch out. She wants to know for the book," warned Grace.

And from there on, I got nothing serious out of either of them. "I don't care that you don't look like me, but I do care that you're so old," said Grace, with a teasing smile.

This prompted Lucy to go one better. "I mind that you're single, and I mind that you're old," she said, "but I don't mind being adopted because it makes a really good story for my college essay." That's what I got for raising them with my sense of humor.

"But wait: Does that really upset you, honey?" I never knew when to stop when ahead.

"Nooo, Mooom," Lucy droned with exaggerated patience. "It...does... not...upset...me..." She drew each word out to twice its normal length in an effort to let me know how exasperating I could be. "It's just annoying.

Everyone always asks, 'Is that your Mom? Why's she so old? Why doesn't she look like you?' It's just annoying."

And then, as if on cue, a little blond child came over and started in on exactly the inquiry that Lucy found so tedious: "Are these your kids? Why don't they look like you?" And then she went one better. "Where's their dad?"

"They don't have one," I said through gritted teeth, in a warning tone that she was not too young to pick up.

And she went away muttering under her breath, "That's not possible." From the mouths of babes: our family isn't supposed to exist. Small wonder Lucy and Grace think that, however physically excruciating, it will be a lot easier to have babies the traditional way.

CHAPTER 12

Learning to Love China From Afar

We were trapped in the kind of gridlock that looked like it might last for days when eight men trotted past with a body. From the icy sanctuary of the company minivan, we gawked as sweat-drenched mourners manhandled a shrouded corpse through the tangle of goats and tuk-tuks blocking traffic in front of us. The deceased was well on his way to eternity before Grace and Lucy recovered from the culture shock of our first morning in New Delhi.

For Grace, the cadaver was the last straw. She had been sure she'd detest India even before we got there, but the corpse made it official. Beggars clutched tumors the size of infants. Growth-stunted preteens did treacherous cartwheels between the tangled lanes of traffic while knocking insistently on our tinted windows for filthy five-rupee notes (less than a dollar). It was too much reality for a squeamish child who had never wanted for anything but an iPhone 6, despite her tough beginnings.

I pointed out that back home in Shanghai, she regularly stepped over limbless and skull-caved beggars on the way to the McDonald's near her school, and they didn't put her off her double cheeseburger. But for some reason she found Indian destitution a lot more upsetting than the Chinese version. Not to mention the fact that McDonald's India didn't even have double cheeseburgers. Poor people everywhere and nary a beef burger to be found: that was Grace Waldmeir's definition of Hades.

"China doesn't have half-dead people lying by the side of the road," she exclaimed indignantly afterward.

And before I had a chance to point out that that was about the most positive thing she'd ever said about her homeland, Lucy chimed in with "This gives me new respect for China."

We were hiding from the sun on the deep cool verandah of the Raj-era guesthouse of an *FT* colleague, where we stayed in Delhi. There was a full English breakfast on the tablecloth before us and bottomless cups of extra-strong tea, and deep bowls of ripe guavas and paw-paws were to be had for the asking. Barefoot middle-aged servants, a husband and wife pair, padded silently to and fro as we debated the relative merits of India and China.

"You can thank the one-child policy for the fact that Chinese beggars aren't so in your face and desperate," I pointed out, perhaps tactlessly. But Grace and Lucy had no trouble accepting that the same brutal birth restrictions that landed them on the side of the road in a box also helped spare their motherland the kind of poverty they saw all around them in India. Anything to avoid so many beggars.

This was not an academic discussion: our immediate future as a family, at the time, depended on it. *The Financial Times* had told me that it was time to leave Shanghai, but there were precious few other postings to choose from. So we were considering Delhi; or rather, I was. Grace and Lucy had made it crystal clear that India was the last place on earth they'd like to live—lower down the totem pole even than China. And I had made it just as clear to them that we really didn't have much choice. If they wanted to go to college, I needed to have a job, and after thirty-five years with the *FT* by then, I wasn't about to look for a new one. We would need to go where the *FT* sent us.

"But wait a minute," I spluttered. "You guys always say you hate China. Why the sudden affection for Shanghai?" My voice had gone up just enough to send the staff scurrying back to the scullery, though they hadn't a clue what we were arguing about. In fact, neither did I. Hadn't I always wanted the girls to give their homeland a break? Did it matter if they could only learn to love China by detesting India?

But it would matter if we ended up living in India. Personally, I loved the subcontinent. I loved the heat, the dust, and the chaos of the roadside; I loved the warmth of the colors and of the people. Maybe it was just that I really like poor countries—poorer even than China—better than rich ones. Not exactly something to be proud of.

But after eight years of fighting a losing battle defending China in the family, my heart sank at the notion of having to do the same for India. In fact, we spent our whole week in India arguing, with increasing sullenness from the kids and rising stridency from me, about whether India was or was not livable. It didn't help my case that three of our four hosts were down with suspected dengue, or "bone-breaking," fever at the time. At least that was a pestilence Shanghai didn't have.

Even bribery failed: a five-hundred-dollar-a-night hotel room with a clear view of the Taj Mahal and staff straight from Merchant and Ivory just left the kids whining about the poor choice of TV channels. Our clichéd Taj-Mahal-in-the-background family photo is one of the saddest testaments I've ever seen to a Waldmeir family vacation: Lucy's narrow shoulders slump forward, the corners of her eyes turn down in dejection, and her lower lip juts out in a toddler-worthy pout. Grace just squints and clutches her water bottle for dear life. Even wonders of the world couldn't cheer them up.

Luckily for Grace and Lucy, the *FT* nixed our putative Delhi move shortly afterward anyway. But at least the Taj Mahal and an Indian cadaver achieved what I'd failed to accomplish in the previous decade of trying: they gave my children a reason to be proud of China.

Grace had just come home from school, and I didn't quite know how to tell her we were not moving to Delhi; we were not moving to Sydney, which we'd been discussing as an option after Delhi; we were moving to a country whose capital we could not even pinpoint on a map.

My sixteen-year-old beauty, clad in faded, stained school uniform and her trademark long lank dirty hair, slumped onto the dog-hair-laden coverlet of the maternal bed and said just one word: "Where?"

"Indonesia," I said, still in shock from the news delivered by unwelcome phone call from London only moments before.

"Well, we knew we couldn't count on Australia," said this child, who regularly interspersed teen irresponsibility with just such flashes of remarkable maturity. From her Victoria's Secret figure to her effortless physical and mental strength, I reflected again that her birth parents must be remarkable specimens. She certainly didn't get any of that from me.

"Some of my Twitter friends are from Indonesia. I'll ask them what it's like." She perked up, jabbing away at her outmoded iPhone.

The response was immediate: "The people are nice, and the food is good."

She said everything would be fine so long as Grace did not go to the school I had in fact just picked out for her (having become an expert on Javanese schooling in the forty-five minutes since the call came).

"Why not?" I asked, thinking, Could this day possibly get worse?

Google promptly let us know that two teachers from that school had been jailed the previous year for abusing preschoolers, to which I, unbelievably, replied, "Oh, it's probably OK then, honey. They won't sexually molest the big kids; you can defend yourselves."

Grace, incredulous, inquired, "Did you seriously just say that it's fine so long as they only abuse toddlers?" And we both collapsed in laughter.

Poking around further, we unearthed a digital report of the Indonesian judge's reasoning for finding the teachers guilty. They only had sex with their wives once a month and didn't masturbate, so they must have needed another sexual outlet in the form of students, the judge concluded. We might not have known where Indonesia was, but we could both see it might be entertaining to live in a country where reasoning like that passed for logic.

And then a week later, Lucy crept into my room at dawn, the air still redolent of Dumpling the dog, who came out from under the bedcovers to wonder at her unexpected presence. She plonked down in a chair, her back to me.

"I'm being mean to people," she said, when I gently probed for what was wrong.

"Are you upset about leaving?" I was struck by a pang of guilt for worrying more about the logistics of this complicated move than about its effect on my beloved children. She gave what I just barely recognized as nonverbal assent; Lucy normally never discussed her feelings, even monosyllabically. "Is it because you'll miss China?" There was nothing ambiguous about her reply to that one: a loud guffaw. She certainly liked China better than Grace but not enough to be missing it before it was even light outside.

I realized that Lucy would not so much miss China as the whole package of her life in Shanghai: an international school full of friends and teachers who had known her since she was a gap-toothed seven-year-old, an *ayi* who adored her and spoiled her just like a Chinese grandmother, a home that was the only one she could clearly remember, and food that her stomach preferred to any other on earth. Maybe that added up to missing China, though she would never admit it. Maybe China was so much a part of her by then that she wouldn't even miss it until it was gone. Maybe absence would make my girls' Chinese hearts grow fonder, I thought. Maybe it would have that effect on all of us.

**Our last family photo with nanny Lu Mudan and
dogs, before leaving China in 2016**

"I want the one with the staircase." We'd spent the day looking at scores of houses in Jakarta, and Grace loved everything she saw: the seven-bedroom mansion with servants' quarters larger than our entire house in Shanghai, a succession of five-bedroom tropical palaces with cool tile floors and plunge pools, and at the end of the day, the house with the sweeping bronze staircase that might have been built for Ginger Rogers. We were on the verge of agreeing to rent that one, which, like all the rest, required that the *Financial Times* make a down payment of nearly $100,000, the equivalent of two years rent, in advance. I felt so guilty about uprooting the kids in the middle of high school—Lucy would be a sophomore and Grace a junior when we moved—that I was willing to bust the rent budget as a consolation prize. (We'd have to pay after the fact, even if the *FT* paid the up-front deposit.)

Grace was spending so much time helping me arrange the complicated move—getting our two Chinese dogs into Jakarta was proving to be nearly impossible—that she often joked that she was "like a husband."

"What did that make Lucy?" I asked.

"Lucy is more like a...well...like a gerbil," she decided: like a pet who was cute and well loved, but not much help with anything. Lucy, for her part, had learned long ago that when Mom and Grace were busy making plans, especially plans that involved our many long overseas trips, like our RV trip through Australia and New Zealand or the trips to India and Indonesia, she should just pretend she wasn't there. Otherwise, someone might ask her to dump poop from the RV or do the electricity hookup. Gerbils don't have to do that.

In Jakarta, Lucy had predictably left me and Grace to get on with the house search. She expressed her views in no uncertain terms on schooling, though. After she scored very creditable 92 percent on the entrance test at one school, she pronounced that she didn't want to go there because all the other students must be idiots. She also objected to the move from her Chinese British international school where the curriculum was UK-style to a Javanese American school where the courses were from the United States.

Luckily for her, all that became moot when we didn't move to Indonesia.

We almost did, but not quite. Within three short weeks of learning the map coordinates for Jakarta, we had a lease on a mansion, had all but hired four Indonesian servants with whom we had no common language, and had gained admission to the school that provoked such creative jurisprudence from an Indonesian judge. I was patting myself on the back for hyperefficiency—and the kids on the head for keeping remarkably open minds to the idea of moving to yet another third-world poverty trap—when the *FT* pulled the plug on Jakarta, too. Another month, another foreign posting failure, but if not Delhi, Sydney, or Jakarta, then where?

Grace was distraught. By the time she'd found out that Indonesian McDonald's not only serves beef but delivers and that we could afford the Ginger Rogers house, she was itching to learn Bahasa Indonesia, the local language. It was a good thing we test-drove India first; she found plenty in Jakarta to compare favorably with Delhi. Scooter drivers wore helmets there, she pointed out right away; motorists sometimes ceded right of way; and she could wear spaghetti straps without getting gawked at. "I'm gonna be fine with it," she announced after about as much familiarity with the place as had caused her to detest India.

So she was nearly as annoyed as I was to hear that we weren't moving after all. "I want to leave China. I never wanted to be here in the first place, and I was looking forward to getting out—even to Jakarta," she said, dejectedly heading back to school in Shanghai, the city she had never learned to love.

Ironically, right before we starting touring Asia looking for a new home, I had been reflecting on how much I loved the one I had: Shanghai. It had taken me years to get used to it, but get used to it I did. I'd learned to love China first for its food and then for its countryside and its people. Finally, I learned to love it on its own terms. Big dirty Shanghai was never my favorite part of the motherland, but I even came to love that, too.

On one level, I simply loved stepping outside my door and finding myself in such an alien country—exactly what I had least liked at the beginning. Go figure.

I loved the sheer vibrancy of the middle kingdom, where one could take even the thinnest slice of a street scene and find it teeming with life. Think

Bruegel, with Chinese characteristics. I loved the fact that I could walk a few hundred yards to the neighborhood "wet market" and get a haircut, a tooth pulled, or a Styrofoam container full of lard-laced *shengjianbao* to take home to delight the girls. And I loved the way that, by then, everyone complimented me on my Chinese, which probably never exceeded elementary school level but was just fine for communicating on a daily basis. And when it came to issues relating to adoption, I could even hold fairly sophisticated conversations—I'd had so much practice at it.

I had always loved being a celebrity on the cheap. Back in Ghana in the 1980s, Ghanaians regularly told me I looked like the late Lady Diana. Nobody ever told me that back in the United States (since I look nothing like her). Shanghai suited me down to the ground by the time I found out that we would have to leave it.

Still, by the time the *FT* canceled our Jakarta move, I'd been preparing to leave for nearly a year, subtly severing the ties that took so long to build. I didn't have the energy to rebuild a new life in China yet again. The idea of staying on exhausted and depressed me.

But Lucy couldn't stop grinning. She had liked Jakarta, but she liked the idea of spending another three years with her school friends in China even better. As she pointed out later, Shanghai is a very teen-friendly city. Every weekend, her friends walked to the local mall, just down the road from the wet market, where there was so much more than shopping to be done. "In that one mall, there's an arcade, there's karaoke, there's an ice rink, mini golf, movies, and everything from Korean barbecue to hot pot to Dairy Queen, not to mention shopping!" she told my extended family when we were in the United States once on home leave. "And you can walk down the street at two a.m., and you'll be safe."

But Grace and I were despondent, so we turned our minds to what would cheer us up: a new house in Shanghai? Couldn't afford one. A car and driver? Ditto. A trip to Australia? That would just depress us. We'd planned three elaborate moves to three exotic foreign countries in the space of less than six months. The last thing we were psychologically prepared for was just to stay put. And then, within days, we had another overseas destination in our sights:

unbelievably, the *FT* was offering us a chance to leave the motherland and head back home to America.

"Sometimes I forget I'm Chinese…and when my friends refer to white people, I say, 'Hey, I'm a white person!'"

After eight years of worrying about how to teach my kids to be Chinese in China, I had to start worrying about how to help them learn to be Chinese in America. Luckily, I'd already asked their adopted Chinese compatriots what it was like to grow up Asian in America. The answer seemed to be that they hadn't noticed.

It was the summer before we were supposed to leave China, and I was asking the oldest of Grace's cohort of adopted friends what she thought of growing up Asian in the United States. She was an exquisite beauty with exactly what Westerners think of as classic Asian features—and which Chinese, many of whom prefer their beauties round eyed, ironically fail to prize. But as she told us over sushi in a Japanese restaurant in Maryland one day, she neither felt Chinese nor associated with anyone ethnically Chinese at her school—in an area near Washington, DC, that had a large proportion of newly emigrated Chinese professionals. She hung out with whites.

Which was probably not surprising. Our children had whiteness thrust upon them by virtue of being raised by white parents. Small wonder that many of them—even including Grace, raised more than half her life in China—thought of themselves as blond at heart. "We're bananas," one of them said when I sat the Yangzhou girls down next to the swimming pool during our last reunion before moving back to the United States. She used the term that refers to Asians who look yellow but feel white and happily applied it to herself.

I asked another whether she was proud to be ethnically Chinese. "I'm fifty percent German, ten percent Irish, and then, like, the rest just European," she said, but those were the roots of her adoptive parents. Talk about forgetting you're Chinese; it didn't even occur to her that her genes were unadulterated Asian.

I was trying to keep all this casual, lobbing my questions at the assembled Yangzhou girls and their little sisters from inside an inner tube as I floated ponderously around the Mueller family pool. But none of the girls seemed to know any of this could be contentious or painful. They were itching to get back to the Wii, to find out which of them was better at virtual bowling.

But I wanted to know. Did any of them wish they were actually born white? The consensus was no. "I like my skin color better—you know, Asians are pretty hairless. And all my friends are like, 'Oh, I hate my hair. I wish I had your hair because it's so easy.'" She'd found her own way to celebrate Chineseness.

Perhaps not surprisingly, the only kids who seemed to have given this ethnicity stuff much thought were my own, and what they said left me wondering if it would not truly have been better to leave them in total ignorance. "I'd rather people know I'm adopted than that they think I'm Chinese," Grace said, primarily because she knew those were the words I would least like to hear from her lips. She later explained that pointing out she was adopted was the best way to defend her Americanness, which was never accepted at face value as it would have been if she were truly the blonde she felt like inside.

"I tell people straight up. When they ask me where I'm from, I say 'I'm adopted' because it's too complicated otherwise to explain it. Because I look fully Chinese. I say, 'I'm American, but I was adopted from China.' I just make sure that they know I'm American." Back when she was little, Grace had an adopted friend whose mother, when asked where the child was from, would say "Takoma Park" (a Washington suburb). Maybe it was time to accept that Grace would really rather be from Takoma Park—or at least she said so in the teen years, when being different is never pleasant.

But it was time to head off to a new life in a country where, for once, I would fit in and they would not. In the United States, their identity as Americans would never be solid and unquestionable in the way that mine (or a blonde's from Takoma Park) would be. In the future, as soon as I uttered a word in my Midwestern twang, strangers would accept me as American. When my teens spoke up with the self-same accent, people would ask why they looked so Chinese. My kids would always be presumed foreign until proven otherwise. And living in China for so many years, ironically, may have made that truer, rather than less so.

For while Grace said she felt white in her soul, it wasn't her soul that Americans were seeing. It was her almond eyes and straight black hair, badges of an ethnicity that she would bear for the rest of her life, however rudely she might reject it. She and Lucy became accidental Americans in the instant of their adoption. It saddened me to think they would have to spend the rest of their lives proving that they deserved that label.

But it didn't sadden them, thank God. Grace's English teacher in her international school in Shanghai once suggested she write an essay focusing on the fact that she looked Chinese but felt American. She peddled him some guff about being conflicted about her identity and then came home to laugh about it. "I'm really not worried about it at all, I just said that because I had to write something," she confided as we sat around watching *Friends* reruns so old that Jennifer Aniston wore shoulder pads.

The teacher also asked Grace to write about how the term *mother* can mean something other than the literal meaning of the person who gave birth to you. This bothered Grace about as much as that family tree so many years before. She couldn't care less how little outsiders understood about our unusual family.

Nothing about us had ever been "normal." I was too old, too white, and too single to be a normal mom, and she was too Chinese and too young to be my normal child. But out of that, we constructed a family that is, in the view of the three of us at least, as imperfectly normal as they come: loving (most of the time), tight knit (some of the time), and even communicative (occasionally). We have always collectively thought it's amusing that the rest of the world thinks adoption matters to how we feel about one another. Having no father matters, being Chinese possibly matters, living in a country where some of us fit in and others didn't made a difference. But adoption was always the least of our worries. Or maybe that's what all adoptive parents like to tell themselves.

For some children do reject adoptive parents in the end. A small but vocal proportion of Korean-American adoptees has spurned their adoptive parents and returned to Korea, hoping to repossess the culture stripped from them by adoption. Since many of them do not speak Korean—and since they, like my kids, were raised as honorary whites—they often find themselves no more at home in Korea than in Kansas. Many vocally condemn international adoption for landing them in this no-man's-land.

Do they have a point? I asked my kids before we left China. Grace let me off the hook right away. "Would they rather have grown up in an orphanage?" she asked dismissively.

Lucy, who was far more interested in whether her orthodontist appointment the next day meant she could skip first period at school, nonetheless took the topic more seriously. "I think they're right to go back and live in Korea," she tossed over her shoulder with absolute conviction on her way to wash her thick black hair. "Because that's where they look like everyone else, unlike in America where they look weird."

"Wait a minute," I spluttered "The fact is they don't fit into either place. They can't speak Korean, and they don't look American. They say that proves international adoption is just plain wrong." And then in a very small voice, I added, "Do you agree with them, Lulu?"

"I do feel more comfortable in China. I feel like it's more my home," she said. "But those parents should just have taken their kids to live in Korea. Then they wouldn't have this problem," and I heard the click of the bathroom lock to signal the subject was closed. Was that a tacit endorsement of the whole Waldmeir sinicization project? That may not have been what Lucy meant—and even if she meant it then, she might not still have meant it after her shower—but I was ready cling to any proof, however slender, that it had been a good idea to move our family to China. I've got a lifetime to think otherwise.

Grace and I were on our way to buy a scale to weigh the life that we had built for ourselves in the motherland. It was time to ship our Chinese life back home to America, and I was still fishing for clues about how the Waldmeirs-to-China project had affected her.

"You know I never really left America in the first place," Grace said, having long ago perfected naughty throwaway lines like that as the best way to shut me up when I started asking how her Chineseness was coming along.

"But is there anything you'll miss?" I asked, in that wheedling tone that was always her clue to start bugging me.

"Yeah," she began, pausing for effect. We were hurrying through the light acid rain that passed for spring in Shanghai, where air pollution, even on a good day, seldom approached the World Health Organization's safe limit for humans. "I'll miss McDonald's and Forever 21, they're better in China than in America," she said. "The fries are saltier here 'cuz the Chinese haven't got all healthy yet." And the Forever 21 Shanghai flagship store, as befits a rag merchant to 23 million people, was just plain bigger. So it came to me in a flash: I would be the last to know what effect China had had on my beloved Chinese daughters. It just wasn't information to be had for the asking.

Soon Grace and I were back home, pawing through the detritus of a life lived in the dirt and grime and heavy metals of a big polluted third-world city: everything we owned was gritty with it. After a few hours of packing, my hands were chapped from the constant compulsion to wash it all off.

Lucy refused to help. She escaped, whenever she could, to the familiar pleasures of arcade and karaoke, Korean barbecue and *shengjianbao* at the mall, and she spoke even less, which is saying something, since her fifteen-year-old self was already firmly monosyllabic. Only later would she tell me, "It felt like you were throwing away our childhood." Even the discolored jewelry box, caked with Shanghai grit, that we had brought from the United States and neither she nor Grace had opened since we moved in eight years before, the one clogged with tangled elastic hair ties snagged on dime store rings. "All that stuff felt like home," she told me later. And it felt like I was throwing home away.

But for me and Grace, it was just junk that needed dumping, especially when we unearthed a slate-colored plastic bin from beneath the fake Christmas tree to find it full of moldy Chinese New Year decorations, including the finger-paint-bedecked dragon costume they used as toddlers. There was money for the dead all stuck in a block by humidity, red envelopes turned a nasty shade of crimson, and tattered couplets that I once hung upside down in our house in Maryland. And then, with a sigh to chase away the cultural obligations of a lifetime, I tossed the whole musty mess into a pristine black trash bag and closed the door on the well-meaning celebration of fake Chinese festivals, forever.

But I was throwing away more than dragon costumes. I was sloughing off the unspoken guilt that drove us to China in the first place: for the ancestors, the past, the culture, and the history, ripped from my children at the moment I became their mother. For depriving two families of a perhaps beloved child, just so I would not have to end my life childless. I felt I had paid my dues to my children, to their Chinese birth parents, and to China. Finally.

But I was certainly not washing my hands of the place I had learned to love, slowly, reluctantly, but oh, so deeply in the end. For whether Grace and Lucy liked it or not, China would always be their motherland. However many times they renewed their American passports, however many US elections they voted in, however many US driver's licenses or marriage licenses or even divorce decrees that they procured, a part of them would be forever China. And a part of me would be, too. They would always be my forever children, and all of us would always be just that little bit Chinese. That's why I moved our family to China: to honor that Chinese part of all of us.

I had tried to teach them to understand, to appreciate, and ultimately, to be proud of that part. Maybe all I did was put them off it forever. But I was finished trying to teach them how to be Chinese in China. It was time for them to teach themselves to be Chinese in the world.

For they would soon be all grown up and living in a two-power world where they would either see themselves as caught in a no-man's-land between two behemoths or stand strongly with a foot in each camp and help the rest of us straddle the divide. Maybe they would thank me for giving them that choice. They might hate me for it, or they just possibly might never care. Perhaps I'd be long gone by the time they even made up their minds. Maybe these two lost daughters of China would only grow into their Chineseness over decades.

But I knew it wouldn't take me that long. After eight years of loving and hating the air, the crowds, the chaos, the coarseness, I already knew for sure that a corner of my foreign heart would be forever China. I just hoped I wouldn't always be the most Chinese member of the family.

EPILOGUE

"POLICE SAID THE STUDENT WHO was shot was being treated at an area hospital. They provided no details on the shooters." The radio had broken into its programming with a bulletin on what it said was a school shooting in progress. I had just caught the end of it, turning on the car radio after coming out of the Walgreens around the corner from our new American home, a fourth-floor walk-up apartment near the shores of Lake Michigan in Evanston, Illinois, a prosperous suburb of Chicago. I'd just been sitting there savoring the joy of being able to tell the difference between shampoo and conditioner after years of baffling Chinese hair-care aisles. But at least Shanghai didn't have school shootings, I reflected.

I didn't, at first, think the news bulletin had anything to do with me. Probably something down on the city's notoriously violent south side, I smugly assumed. Still, I grabbed my phone to google the unfamiliar number of Grace and Lucy's school to give the office a call anyway. At their old school in Shanghai, which they attended from second to tenth grades, I not only had the office on speed dial, but the staff recognized me by voice. (Adoption made us memorable.) The new school where Grace and Lucy had started class only two weeks before had nearly 3,500 students and twelve gyms and was the largest high school under one roof in the United States. We weren't exactly celebrities there.

But before I could dial, the phone jangled with the extra-loud chorus that meant a text from one of the kids. "They just had an announcement that we should stay inside today because there was a shooting on Lee Street." Welcome to America. Lee Street was our new neighborhood.

I could see, from the grayed-out dots on the texting screen, that Grace was still typing. I held my breath. "They don't think the shooter's headed this way, though. Can you pick me up at 2:15 after school?" Grace, who had already been told that the shooting did not, in fact, involve a student and was several blocks away from the school, was primarily concerned with wheedling a ride out of me so she didn't have to take the public bus home. Soon my phone was ringing and buzzing and pinging all at once, as the school delivered e-mail and text and recorded phone alerts about the incident. They said students had never been in any danger. But Lee Street was only a block from our new home, so that wasn't much consolation.

The violence and the food: those were the things that most dismayed us about being back "home." China had the best of both those things: the low crime rate of a police state and the cuisine of a culture that had been practicing it for five thousand years. America had democracy and hamburgers. Some of us were struggling with the trade-off.

"People used to ask me 'Why is your Chinese so bad?' and now they ask me "Why is your English so good?"" Lucy was just plain fed up with looking like what she was not and failing to look like what she was. Within days of starting school in the United States—even before the shooter incident—she was despondent. She even stopped singing. For years, she had tortured me by singing along to pop tunes on her iPod, the same song over and over again, but when we moved to America, she terrified me by ceasing that torture.

"I want to go to boarding school," she announced on day two of the new school year. "My friends back home"—by which she meant Shanghai—"say boarding schools do a much better job of making new students feel welcome."

That blindsided me. Back in China, a Chinese friend had recommended I put my girls in boarding school at the ages of seven and eight, as all hers boarded during the week from age five. But I could scarcely bear the idea of parting with them at eighteen. I only had Lucy for three more years until college as it was.

While I was figuring out how to put that into words, and throw in a dash of "We can't afford it anyway honey," Lucy spat out the rest of her lament. "Precisely one person has said hello to me so far. No one shows me around, I have no one to sit with at lunch, no one even knows I'm a new student!" she wailed as she dumped her heavy backpack disconsolately on the new couch. It didn't help that Dumpling and Huahua, our two beloved Chinese strays, were still back in China and not there shedding on the sofa waiting for her, as they would have been in Shanghai.

Being Chinese did not make things any easier. "Everybody asks me where I'm from, and when I say I moved here from China, they say 'You speak such good English,'" Lucy said, her tone high and nasal and filled with vitriol. "Even when I tell them I'm adopted, they're like, 'Still, great English!' and I'm like, 'Yeah, OK." She rolled her eyes. She would later learn to retort "You have pretty good English, too." But back then, she was simply outraged that most of her classmates "haven't even been outside the United States!" as though this were a personal affront.

And she hated the way people "tiptoe around the fact that I'm adopted. They sort of pity me or show that they feel bad even if they don't want to, and it's really annoying." Both my girls had always hated other people's ideas about adoption. "It doesn't bother me at all to be adopted, but it bothers me that it bothers other people," said Grace, though she was temperamentally less inclined to lose sleep over it. "It annoys me that people are, like…" She adopted a weedy whisper. "Can I ask you about this?"

"They see us as different when we aren't," Lucy chimed in angrily.

She directed most of that anger at me, as well she might since I was the home-wrecker in the family. "I didn't even realize China was my home until you took it away from me," she hissed. I could hear her, through the thin wall that separated her bedroom from mine in our tiny three-bedroom apartment that was a poor excuse for a new home. In the predawn hours of every day, she would call her friends back in China, and I would hear her laughing. And then she'd come home from school, and they'd be asleep, and there would be no one to chat to, and she would stop laughing. For the first three months of our new life in America, our apartment was filled with the sound of Lucy not singing and not laughing.

And then it was Grace's seventeenth birthday, and she didn't even know enough people to invite to a party. At their old, cramped Shanghai international school, where grades four through twelve were crammed in together, the whole cafeteria would erupt in singing if anyone had a birthday. But the new school had four cafeterias, and Grace was still sitting alone at lunch. "I don't care, Mom. I'm just so glad to be back in America," she told me, as we tried to reenact the birthday cake tourism we had perfected in Shanghai, hitting all the cake emporia of Evanston. She had decided that if she didn't have enough friends for a party, she would just buy a huge cake and make friends by handing it out in the hallways at school. So though she feared the violence and hated the solitary lunchtimes, she was still settling in far better than anyone else in the family. This kid must have some phenomenally well-adjusted genes, I thought.

She threw herself into Americana like a prisoner of war released from cultural captivity overseas. When the Chicago Cubs, our northside Chicago home team, headed to the World Series for the first time in 108 years, she became a baseball nut overnight. Many of the games were played on weekend nights, when she had a part time job—appropriately—at a Chinese restaurant. So she followed the play-by-play on the MLB app on her phone, sneaking a peak at it under the counter whenever the takeout phone line wasn't ringing. And when I picked her up after work, I was sure to have the car radio already tuned to the sports station. For the final game in the nail-biting series, she had the night off, so we watched it together, with me spitting invective at the screen at every wild pitch or passed ball. Throughout that frustratingly weak Cubs game, Grace defended her team's every move, even sending me out at the seventh inning stretch to buy a Cubs jersey for her to wear to school the next day. And when the Cubs implausibly clinched the game and the series in the tenth inning, she decided to skip school to attend their victory parade with an estimated five million of her new compatriots in Chicago.

Their new school could not have been more different from the old in another way, too. The student body was evenly split between whites and

African Americans/Hispanics; there were almost no Asians and a very large sprinkling of gay, transgender, and gender-neutral kids, too. At the old school, most everyone was ethnically Asian, or half-Asian, and pretty much everyone identified as straight, at least in public. The handful of white students stuck out.

"A guy tried to tell me in class today that gender doesn't exist," said Grace, going on to say this was conventional wisdom in the student body. "So I thought to myself, 'Dude, you've got a penis, and I've got a vagina, so what's your point exactly?'"

But, ironically and unexpectedly, the school's obsession with diversity ended up helping Grace see the point of all those years in China. "I'm fine with it if they see me as Chinese 'cuz it makes me different. It makes me interesting, cultured, not boring. Now I'm embracing it 'cuz it makes me different from all these white folk here in America." What? Was that an endorsement of the China project? "I hated living in that dirty-ass place that I come from," said Grace. I guessed I'd have to wait longer for the ticker-tape parade celebrating me as the world's most culturally aware parent.

"They had their chance at my liver." We were having an early lunch to celebrate my father's eighty-sixth birthday back in my hometown of Detroit. Dad; my stepmother of more than forty years, Marilyn; my thirty-something sister Lindsey; and the Chinese girls they all cherish were gathered in a private room at a local restaurant because it made it easier for all of us elderly people to hear one another talk. As happens in our family, where adoption and all its trimmings have never been off limits as a subject of polite conversation, we'd stumbled onto the question of what would happen if one of the kids' birth grandparents needed a liver transplant.

"We're going to volunteer at our orphanages back in China this summer," Lucy had announced, like other kids would fill in grandparents about a stint at summer camp.

"Oh yes?" Grandma inquired politely.

But before anyone could compliment them on their compassionate desire to give back to those less fortunate, Lucy admitted the real reason. "Yeah, we figure it will look good on our college applications."

And then Grandma asked if they were going to try to find their birth parents while they were there. And Grace piped up with a version of the old concern I had always had about taking on unwelcome obligations to blood relatives. "What if somebody in the family needs a liver transplant?"

Others clearly found it hard to follow that logic, not having been party to our many years of family discussions on that topic, so Lucy decided to cut it short there. "They had their chance at my liver. They should have thought of that before they left me by the side of the road," she added, to much hilarity.

It had been four months since school had started, and Lucy had already begun to adjust. She perched on the closed lid of our shared toilet for half an hour every morning drawing on wide black sculpted eyebrows with a heavy pencil that gave her an edgy Goth look. She no longer had so much time to talk to China.

And then a few days shy of her sixteenth birthday, she brought up the topic again in private. We were en route to her weekly Chinese lesson—her choice this time, not mine. Lucy wanted to sit the advanced placement test in Mandarin, but her school didn't offer Chinese at her advanced level, so we trekked downtown every Sunday to a tutor with the broad face of a Chinese peasant, whose English was, crucially, worse than Lucy's Chinese. Lucy was in the back seat, and in the mirror, I could see her black bomber jacket, black cut-out leggings, black top, black eyeliner, and etched black eyebrows, but I couldn't quite make out the expression in her eyes. I knew it wasn't the flippant "They had their chance at my liver" expression, though.

"I want to look for them one day—not now, but one day. If I don't, I'm afraid I'll regret it for the rest of my life," she had just announced. Maybe not looking me in the eye made it easier to say that without making a joke of it. "Would you be threatened by that?" she asked, as we streaked through the gray midwinter streets, rushing to get back in time to pick Grace up for work at the Chinese restaurant.

"Of course not," I protested, wondering if she'd even been listening when I'd encouraged her to think about searching, every year like clockwork. "It would have an impact on lots of people apart from you," I droned, as I had always felt obligated to do. She, reasonably, thought I meant me and Grace. "No, I mean your birth mother, birth father, birth grandparents on both sides, birth siblings, blah blah down the family tree." She was just a teen, but such a choice could mark the rest of her life; I felt I had a duty to point that out.

"Oh, I never even thought of them," she said glumly, as it began to dawn on her that this wasn't some DNA treasure hunt; real lives would be changed.

"There is almost certainly a grandmother involved who pressured or even forced your mother to give you up. Maybe they made peace over that years ago. What if you reopen that wound? Maybe husband and wife made peace over it, and you reopen that wound? And before you land yourself with a familial obligation that lasts fifty or sixty or seventy years—when grandma needs that liver transplant, when you don't want to spend your holidays visiting China—you might want to think about this for more than five minutes," I said, immediately wishing I had stopped at "other people will be affected."

But she wasn't put off. "OK, so we won't start yet. I want to focus on school, and it's a really long process. But I am curious. It's not like I feel like I'm missing anything. It's just that adoption is my go-to research project." Lucy was already planning to write her senior paper on the topic. "So I feel that would give me a whole new perspective on it. I don't feel emotionally attached to it, just really, really curious." And we left the topic for another day, knowing that in our family, it would come up again eventually.

The Yangzhou girls turn 18: from left, Grace, Natalie, Lily and Maya

The four long-haired beauties snuggled up together on the sofa, reenacting the pose of that first Yangster group photo from so long ago in China. They all wore the same T-shirt, bearing a blown up grainy reproduction of their joint baby photo. On the left, just like last time, was Maya from northern Virginia next to Lily from western Maryland, who won the prize for looking exactly like her baby photo, except with hair. To her right was my Grace, lately of the Chicago suburbs, and she was punching Natalie from Chicago, just like she did that last time. Natalie's feet were covered by the tiny square of satin-edged blanket that her parents sent to the orphanage before they even met her and that we all recognized as soon as we saw it. The Yangzhou girls had flown to Chicago or driven across the city so they could be together to celebrate their eighteenth birthday with some of their closest friends on earth: their orphanage mates.

I couldn't help but think back to years of Yangzhou girl photos: lined up like sausage rolls in sleeping bags, flanked by three or four little sisters from China, on the floor of Lily's parents' weekend home in Maryland. Or modeling identical bikinis together at Walmart—or identical prom dresses. Or baiting crab pots together in a tributary of the Chesapeake Bay. In year after year of bathing beauty photos, as they dashed into the surf at the beach at Assateague or Ocean City, I remembered the same eyes, the same smiles, the same ruby lips of that first infant photo back in China. And I teared up, as always, with gratitude for these, my extra Chinese daughters.

"When you think that we are all just, like, adopted together? That's a bond that I don't have with any of my friends. We were all in the orphanage together! Even though we hardly see one another, every time we see one another, we can just start talking about random things, and it's not awkward at all," Natalie marveled. She was shouting across a ten-person dim sum table at our favorite restaurant in Chicago's Chinatown, where we'd gone for a farewell lunch at the end of a weekend where we parents could always find the Yangzhou girls, even in Chicago's crowded Millennium Park, by the sound of their giggles and guffaws.

"When I see friends that I haven't seen since middle school, we have nothing to talk about, but when I get here, we just pick up where we left off. It's not strange," Maya piped up from across the table, between bites of rice-skinned shrimp dumpling.

Grace was sitting next to her, dismembering a pot sticker on the off chance that a shrimp might have crept in among the pork; Grace hates seafood. "I'm super close with my cousins, but it's not like this."

I wanted to know if they ever talked about being adopted, and they all thought that was a dumb idea. Adoption had made at least a cameo appearance in all their college essays—our kids knew a good sob story when they heard it—but Lily admitted right away that "sometimes I forget that I'm adopted," which struck a chord with the others, too. Still, if she ever adopted kids herself, which she said she wanted to do, they would be kids who looked like her, she said; she was tired of people tiptoeing around the topic of adoption, just like my kids.

Maya piped up that many of her friends and classmates were adopted, so she never gave it a thought either way, though she was grateful that it happened when they were babies. "We are living such a better life. I'm grateful," she concluded. A Shanghai taxi driver couldn't have said it better.

"It's something that I know happened, but I don't feel any emotional ties to it. It's in my past. Hakuna matata, I guess!" Lily concluded with her trademark giggle, the one we all learned to love back when, as toddlers, they lined up in front of the TV to watch Lion King movies together. Around us was a restaurant full of extended Chinese families—the kind that look like one another—but I wondered whether they could possibly be any closer than our extended Yangzhou clan.

But the fact remains: some of our Yangzhou family are Chinese, and some are not. How did the girls feel about that, I asked, after coaxing them all to try some of the duck and thousand-year-old egg rice gruel that, to me, tasted most of China. I'd noticed that those of them with almond Asian eyes—Nat and Grace—always struggled to make their eyes look larger in photos, including their graduation photos. But even Lily, who like Maya has round eyes with a Western-style double eyelid, sheepishly admitted "I have an Asian app on my phone that opens my eyes wider for me when I take selfies." To that, we all guffawed, though none of the other Chinese families seemed to notice.

Chinese Americans definitely don't stare at us like real Chinese people do, I thought.

"Seriously, though, guys, what *do* you think of being Chinese?" I insisted. I might never have them in one place again, suitably softened up with soup dumplings.

"Sometimes I forget that I'm Chinese. I feel white because I'm with everyone else who's also white," said Lily, who went on to explain that her school community was all white.

Morgan Distler, who grew up entirely in France with big Yangzhou sister Emma, said she'd been told by friends and a teacher once that she had a Chinese accent. "I felt a bit hurt because I don't even speak Chinese. I could understand it if they thought I had an American accent," she told me by Skype later from Paris. And I thought that just about the only thing harder than growing up Chinese American in the United States would be to grow up Chinese American in Paris.

My kids, after forced immersion in China, inevitably felt the Chineseness more. "I feel half white and half Chinese, but I think society sees me as fully Chinese," said Lucy, the honorary Yangzhou little sister. "I'm sort of a cultural mix, but when I'm just going through the halls in school and people see me, they think 'That's an Asian person.' That's a difference between how society sees me and how I see myself."

By then, Grace was happy to be seen as different, and she tried to explain that to her Yangzhou sisters. "It makes me special to be Chinese. I've embraced it now more than I did in China where I wanted to be white." They had all grown up so differently—on a farm in all-white Western Maryland (Lily), in a multiracial area of the Washington, DC, suburbs (Maya), in an affluent Chicago suburb (Natalie), and far away in Paris (Emma, who couldn't make the reunion)—that I wondered how much they truly had in common on this question. Probably, only time would tell. They would have far more to teach me about being Chinese in America in the future than I would ever have to teach any of them.

What about birth parents? Nat said finding them would be "kinda cool," and Maya said she'd be open to finding biological siblings, but in an offhand tone that made clear this was not an existential burning desire.

"I don't really want to find them," chimed in Lily. "The only thing I'd be interested in is if I have a twin. It's more about who you grow up with than about genetics."

Grace, who'd been through this conversation once too often in our nuclear family, set out more to entertain her Yangzhou sisters than to answer seriously. "I don't wanna find my birth parents 'cuz they are probably poor, and I don't want to visit them in their shack," she said to peals of her sisters' giggles. "I'm just happy that I was adopted when I think what my life could have been like. I would have been really poor and doing rice field stuff." (Clearly, that rice-planting Guizhou trip really scarred her.) "I couldn't plant rice every day, and I wouldn't have a phone." Grace knew what her priorities were, and she wanted to make sure her Yangzhou mates—and everyone else in the restaurant and, for that matter, in China—knew what they were, too.

"There are toddlers running in circles around me, some in Spiderman pajamas and some in Hello Kitty outfits. They're pulling at my arms and begging me to give them all my attention. Giggling as they push each other down a yellow slide, they use their pudgy fingers to trace the outline of a lady bug on the faded wall mural. Little Lily, not yet two, clutches a teddy, and stomps around the room as if she owns it, her pigtails bouncing with every stride. No one would guess that Lily was abandoned by a Chinese road and now lives in an orphanage."

Just as she threatened, Grace had decided that the best sob story for her college essay was an account of her trip with Lucy to volunteer at an orphanage in China at the end of our first year back in the United States. "Some have a hole in the heart or a cleft palate, hard to look at but relatively easy to repair. Others have crippling illnesses like spina bifida or hydrocephaly. But despite their disabilities, they all seem to be having a good time: they love playing with each other and they love having me there to cart them around, hug them, and give them what they miss most, love and attention. My story is not so different from theirs…"

And thus it all rolled out, her story. Lucy planned to do the same thing the next year: milk adoption for all it was worth, hoping it would land her in the Ivy League. For years, they had politely tolerated the pity of their classmates; it was time to put it to work for them.

The first trip back to China that Grace, seventeen, and Lucy, sixteen, made without me, crossing continents and oceans on their own, felt like it closed the last chapter of the China section of our story. Grace came back more convinced than ever that she could never, ever, under any circumstances live in the middle kingdom. And Lucy came back to her well-established new friendships in the United States, saying "I loved my life there in a way that I really just don't love my life in Evanston. I don't think I'll ever have that emotional connection that I have with Shanghai. It really made me who I am. It helped me find the part of me that is Chinese in my identity." And no, I didn't coach her on that answer.

The trip also caused Lucy to reverse a long-held conviction that she herself would never adopt because she didn't want her kids to feel pitied the way she had. "But when we went back to volunteer at the orphanage, my opinion completely changed because I developed bonds and relationships with those kids that I didn't know that I could have. I felt like it doesn't matter how other people see me. It's about how I feel, and I realized I could develop bonds with children who aren't biologically related, and I'd definitely be open to adoption." To me, that felt like a hat trick. The kids had started to get settled in their souls about Chineseness, about adoption, and about parenthood, all for the price of two off-peak plane tickets to Shanghai.

And me? Well, I surprised myself by being about as culture shocked by reimmersion in the United States as I had been all those years ago when catapulted to China. In Evanston, home to hundreds of mainland students at nearby Northwestern University, I often heard Mandarin spoken at Starbucks or the grocery store or the hairdresser. I wasn't surprised at that, but I was surprised to find that I felt most comfortable when surrounded by people who looked and sounded just like everyone back in that place that—improbably— I, too, still considered "home": Shanghai.

So what's the final verdict? How did it all work out, this extended ethnic adventure of ours? Is it possible to teach someone to be Chinese, just by carting them off to China and stuffing them with *shengjianbao* and Mandarin lessons for years? This isn't a question that affects only my kids; it could be an issue for any internationally adopted child. What does it mean to be born into one race and raised by another? Or, for that matter, what does it mean to be Asian American in the United States today? Or Anything American?

Grace and Lucy have changed their tune on this stuff so often that I've lost track. And why shouldn't they? Identity isn't a fixed thing, ethnic or any other kind. I can only confidently say that I may never really know how they feel about being Chinese. I just hope they will figure it out, eventually. Maybe that's why they asked for 23andMe DNA testing kits for Christmas our second holiday back in the United States. Living in China marked them forever. Coming to terms with adoption and Chineseness: that will be the work of a lifetime. But for them, not me.

I'm glad that I gave my children access to that Chinese part of themselves, whether they wanted it or not. And I'm even more pleased that I discovered, almost against my will, that there would always be a Chinese part of me, too. Are we all Americans or Chinese or both or neither? I'm not going to stress about that any more—for any of us. Perhaps that's the most fitting end to our unlikely love story: that we all get to be accidental Chinese Americans together, no matter what we look like.

The End

AUTHOR BIOGRAPHY

PATTI WALDMEIR IS AN AWARD-WINNING author and journalist. She has spent nearly forty years working as a reporter and columnist for the *Financial Times,* reporting from Ghana; Zambia; Nigeria; South Africa; London; Washington, DC; Shanghai; and now Chicago. Raised in Detroit, Waldmeir graduated with honors from the University of Michigan and went on to win a Marshall Scholarship to earn her master's degree at Cambridge University.

Waldmeir's previous award-winning book, *Anatomy of a Miracle: The End of Apartheid and the Birth of a New South Africa,* chronicled the peace deal between white and black in South Africa and the rise of Nelson Mandela. Her latest focuses on a more personal issue. When Waldmeir adopted two Chinese daughters, she decided to move the family to Shanghai to help them keep close to their Chinese heritage. *Chinese Lessons* is a story of identity, race and culture, told through the prism of family.

Printed in Great Britain
by Amazon